Eisenhower on Enlightened Leadership

By Timothy Harrington [©]

Jem Business Media

To James
thanks for inviting me
to join your Board.
Lead like Ike!

Copyright – Second Edition

First edition published February, 2012

Second edition published June, 2012

Acknowledgements

I would like to thank my lovely wife Sherril who has always encouraged and inspired me in every project and endeavor. Sherril inspired me to create this course to meld my love of history with my passion for high integrity leadership.

I would also like to thank my sons Adam and Aron who have put up with visiting every battlefield and World War II museum within driving distance of any family vacation spot.

I would also like to thank my assistant Cornelia Smyth who has a most beautiful spirit and has kept me on track through very hectic and stressful times.

And finally, I would like to give the greatest thanks to my mother, Rita, and my late dad, Bill, who taught me to love history and seek knowledge.

Table of Contents

Chapter

Introduction

I was born during Eisenhower's presidency and was three and half years old when he left office, though I have no memory of that time. As I grew up, I had a vague notion of Eisenhower. But he was the 'old' President. Times had changed. Before I began to study Ike a decade ago, I knew he was a leader in World War II and later became President. Many people know that much about Eisenhower. Yet as I studied Ike, and learned about his leadership style, it became apparent to me that this simple man, had employed a very special kind of leadership. Something I have come to call "enlightened leadership".

Now I don't suggest Ike invented enlightened leadership, but for the first time on a world stage under staggering responsibilities and pressures, a style of high integrity, inclusive, empowering and motivational leadership was demonstrated.

Leadership is actually quite simple. Many people think it is complex or requires God given talents. Certainly, there are leaders who are born that way, but most leaders learn how to lead.

There are different kinds of leaders. Some leaders are dictatorial and compel people to follow through fear and force. Yet other leaders inspire people; people who then continue in the direction of the leader with little guidance or direction from that leader. This kind of leader empowers and rewards staff; holds them accountable with appropriate and sensible consequences. This kind of boss becomes the leader people want to follow.

While leaders of the past were often dictatorial leaders, the leaders of the future will be inspirational leaders; enlightened leaders.

There are many examples of enlightened leaders in recent decades, but I have melded my love for the history and characters of World War II with my passion for high integrity leadership. And in that process, I have been drawn to Ike. Through my studies of the people, politics and incidents of World War II, I continually ran into stories about the Supreme Allied Commander and how he lead and inspired his direct subordinates and even troops he never met. The more I read, the more I said to myself "Wow! This guy is really something. He's using enlightened leadership."

Throughout this book, I have portrayed examples of how Eisenhower practiced enlightened leadership. How he helped people see and remember the vision of the end result he wanted, then how empowered and entrusted subordinates to carry out the work to achieve that vision.

I hope you will enjoy reading Eisenhower on Enlightened Leadership, and perhaps use these methods to practice enlightened leadership in your life.

Chapter 1
An Example of
Enlightened Leadership

The regiment had been in North Africa for over six months. As a fighting force, they had improved. The German *Afrika Korps* had bloodied them badly in early battles, but the Americans had now begun to learn how to fight a war. It was January 1943.

The regiment sat at the farthest eastern advance of the Allied Expeditionary Force in North Africa. This was the front line. The only thing between the regiment and Egypt, a thousand miles to the east, was the formidable General Rommel and the renowned Afrika Korps.

It was a long way to the major supply depots and Allied Headquarters. Those sat four hundred miles to the northwest, in Algiers. The only thing connecting the regiment to Allied HQ and supplies was the lone, narrow paved highway which roughly followed the Mediterranean, and a single ribbon of rusty railroad tracks that paralleled that highway. Aside from that, roads, when they existed at all, were muddy or dusty tracks, depending on the season. The regiment was sitting on the front line in the middle of nowhere and all the men knew it.

Today, it was overcast. No rain had fallen for a week and the troops were beginning to trust it might be gone for good. The weather had fluctuated from too cold, rainy and rivers of mud, to too dusty, sandy and hot enough to heat their K rations in the can. There was nothing comfortable about sitting in a shallow foxhole in this world of sand and mud. Nothing fun at all. Morale was low and no one at HQ seemed to care.

The GI on rear guard duty could see the column of dust miles away. It was caused by three cars coming from the northwest. Whoever was coming in was as obvious to German spotters as to his little outpost.

As the vehicles neared, the GI noted that the lead car resembled a staff car. He radioed the lieutenant and reported the incoming vehicles. The lieutenant asked him to confirm as soon as he could whether it was in fact a staff car. Within a few minutes, the sentry radioed again and reported that it was definitely a staff car; "It's brass of some sort. But I can't tell much more than that yet," he said. The lieutenant told him to get the password then let the vehicles pass, and to radio him ASAP to tell him who was in the car.

Within minutes, the three car convoy pulled up to the sentry and stopped. Because of the dusty windows, the sentry could not make out who was in the car and no flags were flying on the fenders to inform him of the rank. But it was an officer's staff car; that much he was clear.

He walked to the driver's side, gave the password, and awaited the counter sign. The driver looked into the back seat and said "Sir, do you remember the password?" The familiar high pitched, Midwestern voice from the back seat said "No I don't, Sergeant. Maybe we can ask the soldier to let us pass. Tell him we're a little bit lost and we'd like to see his commanding officer."

The voice was unmistakable. The soldier had heard it many times before on Armed Forces Radio. He peered past the driver into the backseat, eyes as wide as silver dollars, mumbled something, then snapped to attention. The driver asked, "Can we go on?"

"Yes sir, sorry sir. I'll let them know you're coming."

As the little caravan rolled toward his platoon and their warren of foxholes, the guard stared for a moment at the back of the lead vehicle, still stunned. Then he ran to the radio. "Lieutenant? You won't believe it, but it's General Eisenhower."

When the cars arrived at the lieutenant's lean-to, word had already spread to the entire platoon. In spite of possible dangers, nearly the entire platoon was leaving their foxholes to come and see the Supreme Commander. Eisenhower got out of his dust-covered car with over fifty curious GIs gawking at him like giddy tourists.

"Sorry I look so crumpled, boys. I just woke up. We drove in from Algiers." He looked at the surprised lieutenant and casually returned his salute. "Hello lieutenant. We're a little bit lost, so I wanted to come by and check in. You know, see how your unit is doing. But we couldn't find your regimental HQ. So I hope I didn't surprise you too much. Maybe you can point us in the right direction after we visit for a bit."

The lieutenant was not sure what to say. Then he stammered, "Sir, you drove four hundred miles from Algiers by yourself? Without an escort?

"Well, not by myself. My driver here is with me. And the other fellows in the other cars."

Ike visiting troops in Tunisia, 1943

"I mean, Sir, there are German patrols and aircraft everywhere. You could have been a target. Four hundred miles, Sir. You must be worn out. We don't have many luxuries here, but can I get you anything to make you more comfortable?"

Eisenhower scanned the GIs and their makeshift camp and smiled. Then he requested his two vices. "Lieutenant. I could use a cup of hot coffee if you have some. And I'm out of cigarettes, I would love a cigarette."

"Sir, the coffee we can get you in a few minutes. But General, we don't have any cigarettes out here. Supply Services says there's no room on the transports for cigs or chocolate. Can you believe that Sir? The men sure miss them. But, that's the way it is. Luckily we have plenty of ammo. The coffee we'll have in just a moment."

The men looked over their commander. The old man looked so normal. And what a smile. Each GI felt like they knew this officer. He didn't seem to use his stars to impress or intimidate them. He just smiled and shook their hands like a proud uncle. He asked them his trademark question: "Where are you from, soldier?" Then he would chat for a few moments. No wonder all the solders talked about "Ike". But what really impressed them was that the Supreme Commander had slept in the backseat of an unescorted sedan driving over four hundred miles across the North African desert just to see them: the soldiers on the front lines.

Before Eisenhower left with directions to the regimental headquarters, he promised to find out about the chocolate and cigarettes. [1]

We'll finish this story, and Ike's clever resolution, later in Chapter 8.

Chapter 2
A Slow Start,
Then a Meteoric Rise

A Very Ordinary Guy

Was Ike Eisenhower a natural leader? No.

He observed leadership, he read about leadership, he practiced leadership, he learned leadership. But he was not born with it.

Why Ike?

Most Americans know very little about Ike Eisenhower. They will likely be able to tell you he was a President, but that may be all. I call Ike the 'Stealth President'. People know very little about him, his military years, or his time in office.

Yet, when I began to study Ike, I began to slowly uncover his genius.

Just before my father crossed over at 92 in 2010, I asked him who his favorite president was. Since my dad was a life-long Democrat who was once very involved in New Deal politics, I expected to hear the names of Roosevelt or Truman or Kennedy. Instead, my dad shocked me and said, "Eisenhower! I really liked Eisenhower. You always felt safe when Eisenhower was President." That recognition of a Republican President from a life-long Democrat said an enormous amount about who Ike was.

When the Allied Powers of World War II needed a unique leader to command a vast array of nations, people, temperaments and weaponry against the greatest military force the world had ever seen, they turned to the most unlikely man: an obscure lieutenant colonel who had never been in combat, much less even seen combat from a distance. In 1941, if the average American or Allied officer drew up a list of the top 100 men they thought likely to become the Supreme Commander of Allied Expeditionary Forces in Europe, Eisenhower would likely not have made the list.

Such a list existed, and fortunately, average officers didn't create it. An insightful and influential man did: Gen. George Marshall, a member of the Combined Chiefs of Staff, as it was known in 1941. Gen. Marshall knew this war would be different than any war the world had ever seen. This would be a war fought with new weapons and would encompass the whole globe. This war wouldn't need a tactician to lead, it would need a superb motivator, planner and administrator. Marshall displayed his unique insight to notice an otherwise obscure fifty-one-year-old lieutenant colonel that had quietly developed unique leadership abilities: Dwight D. "Ike" Eisenhower.

Perhaps you have asked yourself, "What makes one boss, one supervisor, one leader someone for whom I would do anything, and another someone I put up with until you can get the heck out of here?" Well, it's probably not you. More likely, it's the supervisor, the boss, the CEO. Some people are born with natural leadership abilities. Some people are doomed to fail at any attempt at leading.

But the vast majority of people fall in between; the people who, like Eisenhower, can learn to lead.

The great thing about Eisenhower was that he was so ordinary. He displayed no evident qualities of genius that sent him to the top of the pyramid. He didn't have the creative genius of a Walt Disney; or the computer know-how of a Bill Gates; or the financial wisdom of Warren Buffet: he didn't have the acting acumen of a Tom Hanks, nor the military skills of his contemporary George Patton. Eisenhower was an ordinary guy who lived a life of high integrity, made friends easily, worked very hard, and learned to lead. And what he left for all of us is a magnificent roadmap for just that: Learning to Lead.

Eisenhower's style of leadership was far ahead of its time in the 1940s. As a matter of fact, as can be seen by poor leadership in many organizations today, his style is still far ahead of its time. That is why I have termed his style "Enlightened Leadership." It uses the best of humankind to bring out the best in humankind. It is a style of leadership that uses a concept from quantum physics: it vibrates at a very high frequency…like light. Thus, I call it *ENLIGHTENED* leadership.

Slow Start, Meteoric Rise to Top

Ike wasn't born into a life of privilege; he didn't follow in the footsteps of a father who was a military officer or a wealthy businessman; he wasn't continuing a tradition of leadership. As a matter of fact, he was born to a poor family in Denison, Texas in 1890 and lived his youth moving between Denison and Abilene, Kansas. His father was a college graduate, a very rare thing at that time, but nonetheless had a very difficult time making a living. David Eisenhower had failed in several attempts in his own business endeavors and had failed equally as an employee of others. As a matter of fact, Mr. Eisenhower was happiest at home, lying on his bed, reading. Not exactly a model of industriousness or leadership. Therefore, there was rarely much money around the house.

Eisenhower's mother, Ida, was a strong woman with a great heart and hefty doses of integrity. She passed both these traits along to her six sons, including Ike.

Mrs. Eisenhower was a very religious woman. While she did not pass her religion on to Ike and her other sons, she did pass on her strong ethical beliefs and behavior. These were instrumental in Ike's eventual development as a great world leader.

Ike's greatest achievements in his youth were on the sports field. In football, he was a star. In baseball, he was a very hard-working and skilled player. In the classroom, good grades came easily to him, scoring mostly As and Bs.

Upon graduating from high school in 1908, some of Ike's close friends were able to go to college. Ike didn't see how this could happen for him. His finances were dismal. So Ike went to work. College was a dream, but that dream appeared impossible to achieve.

Two years after graduation, when Ike was twenty years old, he learned that the military academies gave a young man a free education if that young man could pass an exam and get a congressman to sponsor him.

West Point and 'Damaged Goods'

With a bit of work, Ike was able to convince a congressman to sponsor him. The young man dreamed of going to the Naval Academy at Annapolis. When he took the entrance exam, he did not score well enough to be accepted at the Naval Academy. Oddly enough, he did score well enough to obtain an appointment to the United States Military Academy. Ike was going to college; he was going to West Point.

Cadet Eisenhower showing his skills on the West Point football team

How is it that West Point wanted him when the Navy didn't? Several historians claim it was not Ike's academic skills or admissions test results that impressed the admissions officers at West Point, but his athletic skills.

And as the years went by, Ike did not disappoint. He made the varsity football team as a second year cadet.

As the football season progressed, Ike began to exhibit his skills as a running back. In the first several games of the season, Ike played extremely well. The New York Times called him "one of the most promising backs in Eastern Football" [2]. He was truly a gifted athlete.

In the seventh game of the season, Ike's sports days came to a sudden end. Ike tore up his knee. With modern medicine, the ligaments could be repaired and with therapy, an athlete today could be back on the field in a few months. In 1912, no such medical technology was available. The only treatment was a cast to his thigh and a hope that the ligaments would heal. They never did.

Ike would never play football or his beloved baseball again. The two sports he loved and lived for he could now only watch. But that hurt too much and for a period he would not even watch those sports.

Ike slipped into a dark mood. He began to smoke in his quarters, go out without proper uniform, and talk back to his cadre (senior cadets). Discipline became a significant issue with Cadet Eisenhower and his demerits began to mount. Some began to question whether Eisenhower was fit for West Point, including Eisenhower.

Ike's knee was a source of constant discomfort. Depression haunted him as a second year cadet. Somehow, Ike made it through his second year.

By his third year, he was beginning to take his studies seriously and eventually turned into a respectable student. In addition, Ike coached. He coached junior varsity sports and proved himself to be a competent coach. His coaching skills would come back to haunt him several times in his career, but at other, perhaps even more important times, they would serve him very well as a leader.

Graduation from West Point would not come easy. It would come only after negotiations with senior administrators at the Academy. The administrators were very concerned about Eisenhower's damaged knee. They did not see how a young man with a gimpy knee could handle the rigors of combat and lead troops. Eisenhower convinced them his knee was good and his body could withstand the rigors of combat as well as anyone's. Though not convinced, the administrators were willing to allow Eisenhower to graduate, on one condition; because of his damaged knee, Cadet Eisenhower would have to sign an agreement stating that he would never apply to nor be eligible for transfer to the cavalry. This agreement would become part of Eisenhower's permanent record, and the information about his bad knee would cast a pall on the rest of his career.

In the Spring of 1915, Ike graduated West Point and was commissioned as a second lieutenant in the United States Army. Lieutenant Eisenhower graduated squarely in the middle of his class, number 61 of 165 graduates. He was no star. However, this class of 1915 would eventually become known as the "Class the Stars Fell On" as it is the class that produced more generals than any other West Point class in history.

When it came to Discipline, Ike fared even worse than his tepid academic achievements. He was rated as 125 out of 165. His history of disciplinary issues and demerits put him only 40 from the bottom. I guess you could say Ike never let the rules limit him.

The Great War: Great Frustration

The Great War was raging in Europe when Ike graduated and was commissioned. America wasn't yet part of the war and would not commit men for another two years. But the graduates of the class of 1915 knew that U.S. entry into the war was inevitable. In 1917, when the American Doughboys began to board troop ships to do their part in the fields of France, many of the young officers from the Class of 1915 were among those embarking for their first real command and their first taste of combat. But not Ike. No one wanted Ike for combat duty because he was "damaged goods". His knee would continue to be an issue. Ike never made it to France during that war. Instead, he busied himself stateside with whatever opportunities he was given.

Between the Wars: More Frustration

When the Great War ended, the military began to demobilize. Eisenhower stayed in the Army, but chances for advancement dwindled as the size of the US military was cut drastically. Ike spent many of the years between 1915 and 1936 stationed at Army camps serving as the camp's football coach. Yes, their football coach. Those skills learned coaching at West Point had caught up to him. Many Camp Commanders saw Ike with his bad knee as "damaged goods," yet they wanted the best football team in the Army. Ike's skill as a coach made him a hot item for Generals who wanted their camp to have a top quality team. While Ike was a man of duty, willing to do anything the Army required of him to his fullest ability, he detested being shipped from camp to camp to coach football.

During these fallow years, Ike also read voraciously, attended many top-quality Army schools (where he did very well), and learned as much as he possibly could. He also spent a great deal of time with his mentor, Gen. Fox Connors, who taught him much about planning and leadership. Despite his label as "damaged goods", Ike aspired for something more. He wanted simply to command soldiers in the field, something, incidentally, he would never do.

In 1936, Ike finally achieved the rank of Lieutenant Colonel. He was sent to the Philippines to serve on the staff of General Douglas MacArthur, America's most famous general. Ike served MacArthur well, even becoming MacArthur's Chief of Staff. Yet, Ike later confided that he learned a lot about leadership from MacArthur. He learned if MacArthur did something, Ike should do exactly the opposite.

Frankly, Eisenhower found MacArthur's leadership style insufferable. According to Eisenhower, MacArthur was a totally self-possessed narcissist. On several occasions, MacArthur took credit for the accomplishments of Eisenhower or others on his staff. And perhaps worse, MacArthur made serious mistakes, and rather than take the blame, he cast the blame on his subordinates, including Eisenhower. Eisenhower saw MacArthur as the epitome of a leader who preferred looking good rather than building a devoted and loyal staff.

Later in the war, Eisenhower stated to a subordinate, "I wouldn't trade one [George] Marshall for fifty MacArthurs." Then Ike paused, laughed and said, "That would be ridiculous. What would I do with fifty MacArthurs?'

Ike asked MacArthur to allow him to return to the US many times. MacArthur would not have it. He could not afford to lose a skilled and talented administrator like Ike. After repeated requests and a breakdown in the relationship between the famous General and his rebellious Chief of Staff, MacArthur finally allowed Ike to return to the US. The two would never have friendly relations again. MacArthur would later refer to Ike as "the best clerk I ever had."

Ike would later say, "I studied dramatics under MacArthur for four years in the Philippines."

World War II Begins: Ike Sees a Dead-End Future

The world was at war yet again. In September of 1939, Germany began invading its neighbors. While Ike had some interesting assignments after returning from the Far East, he could see that the US would eventually join the war against Nazi Germany. Yet, he could also see that he would once again be a desk jockey in this war and would likely never get a chance to lead troops in the field. In the eyes of too many of his fellow officers, he was pigeonholed as a competent officer with excellent planning and administrative skills, but he also had a bad knee and no troop leading experience. Ike didn't want to go into this next war as a desk jockey again.

During Christmas, 1940, Ike told his son that it was becoming more apparent that this 50-year-old soldier was never going to make Colonel. Colonel had been Ike's highest ambition. His greatest fear, as he had confided to his wife Mamie, was that he would never be allowed to lead men, that instead he would be put into war planning. He truly did not want to face another war in a desk job. It was this dreaded possibility of a desk job that caused Ike to start considering retirement.

In so many ways, Ike saw himself as a washed-up, aging officer with limited up-side. He knew that the US Army had over 300 officers superior to him in rank, experience, and recognition. Ike's knee, which was injured in college football, had never fully healed and he, and many other officers, saw Ike as "damaged goods".

America's entrance into the war was clearly inevitable. Ike began to take a greater part in the preparation of the new US troops being rapidly brought into our almost non-existent Army. He was assigned to training troops and planning maneuvers. He began to take on greater and greater responsibility and attract more attention to his planning and administrative skills. With the additional work came some additional recognition. In early 1941, Ike was promoted to Colonel. This was only a 'temporary' grade. A temporary rank meant that after the war, he would revert to his permanent rank of Lieutenant Colonel. Then in October 1941, he was promoted to Brigadier General (one star-temporary). His slow start and slow climb from cadet to Lieutenant Colonel over a twenty-one year period suddenly accelerated beyond Ike's wildest expectations. Ike began to think he might actually have a chance to one day be in charge of a regiment and lead the troops.

Then Something Monumental Occurred

"December 7th, 1941, a date which will live in infamy. The United States of America was suddenly and deliberately attacked by the naval and air forces of the Empire of Japan." These are the words spoken by President Franklin Delano Roosevelt as he appeared before a joint session of Congress on December 8, 1941 asking for a declaration of war on Japan. Congress passed that Declaration of War, and America was again at war.

Five days later Germany and Italy declared war on the United States.

Then on December 12th, 1941, Eisenhower received the dreaded telegram from the War Department. He was ordered to travel to Washington, DC by the fastest means possible. This was a dreaded order because to Ike, it could only mean one thing: he was going to spend the war in Washington, DC as part of the War Plans Department. His dreaded desk jockey job. He was going to be again taken away from leading the troops. The troops he so badly had wanted to lead.

Yet, always a good soldier, he hastily packed a bag, kissed a very disappointed Mamie goodbye and tried to find an air transport. In the confusion of war, with the US Army trying to ship as many troops as possible to defend the West Coast from a potential invasion by Japan, Ike could barely find a seat on any kind of transportation, much less a seat on an aircraft. After several frustrating days, he finally arrived by train in DC and made his way, crumpled uniform and all, to the War Department.

Meeting General Marshall

To his surprise, upon his arrival, he was escorted immediately to the office of the Chief of Staff of the US Army, General Marshall. This surprised Eisenhower because Marshall was the highest ranking, non-civilian leader of the military, roughly equivalent to today's Chairman of the Joint Chiefs of Staff. Eisenhower could not find any reason why this important and powerful man would want to see him so urgently. Ike had only met General Marshall twice very briefly and shaken hands. But these short introductions had occurred years ago. Nonetheless, Eisenhower went as escorted directly to Marshall's office.

Rather than waiting in the outer office as he had expected, he was whisked into Marshall's office. With hardly any preliminaries, and while Ike was still standing in front of Marshall's desk, Marshall asked him, "Eisenhower, how are we going to win this war? What should be our general course of action?"

Ike was taken aback by the question. He stood looking at Marshall for a few moments and realized he was totally unprepared to answer such a question. Because of his experience in the Philippines where the largest concentration of US forces outside the continental US were stationed, he knew something about conditions in the

18

Pacific. Yet, frankly, all he knew of the events of the last few days was what he learned from newspapers, and in the fog of war, they did not reveal much. Further, he had very little information regarding American military readiness and dispositions. Yes, the U.S. had a military, but the entire battle-ready, active duty military consisted of barely 140,000 men in December 1941, though over a million were in training. And nearly half the battle ready military was tied up in the Pacific and most in the Philippines which like Hawaii, had been attacked and was presently still under attack.

Ike looked Marshall in the eye, feeling inadequate with his answer, and said "General, I can't answer your question right now, but if you will give me a few hours, I will try my best to come back with an answer."

Marshall liked this response. He didn't need officers who would tell him what he wanted to hear and he didn't need officers who would deceive him by attempting to buffalo him with a contrived answer. Marshall needed men who could make decisions on their own and who would tell Marshall when they didn't know something and had the wherewithal to find an answer.

He was hoping that Eisenhower would respond to him with an answer like this; and Marshall was prepared. He reached across his desk and picked up a thick file. This file contained the best intelligence available at that moment about the situation in the Pacific and the condition of American forces worldwide. Sadly, it wasn't much information.

He gave the file to Eisenhower, instructed him to use his new office down the hall and told him to report back in two hours.

A Fateful Answer

Ike used the office down the hall, got his ever-present pot of coffee and his pack of cigarettes, and chain-drank and chain-smoked his way through the file. What he learned was very discouraging. The US had, as he had known, a very small active duty military, around 140,000 men. Alarmingly, a large percentage of Army, Navy, Air Corps and Marines were stationed in the Philippines, America's largest protectorate and main staging area in the Eastern Pacific. Like Pearl Harbor on December 7th, the Philippines had been attacked by the Japanese on December 8th, 1941. Ike learned that those forces were fending off Japanese attacks at that very moment. Sadly, they were running out of food, ammunition, fuel and all supplies required to fight a war. Yet because of the severe damage to the American Navy at Pearl Harbor, there was no way the United States could help its people in the Philippines. Nearly 40,000 American service men and women were cut off. They were on their own.

Making matters worse, if worse could be imagined, American training and equipment was inferior to that of the Japanese. Compared to their new enemies in the Pacific and Europe, the U.S. military, what there was of it, was using World War I equipment with World War I training and tactics. The American nation was woefully unprepared for a modern war against aggressive and capable enemies.

Everything that Eisenhower studied was discouraging. Yet, within the few hours allotted to him by Marshall, Eisenhower had begun to formulate a plan.

When he returned to Marshall's office, this man who thought others perceived him as a washed-up, second-rate Lieutenant Colonel, had a surprising answer. Fully knowing the country was in a shooting war with the Empire of Japan in several places in the South Pacific, and fully aware that America's Pacific territorial holdings were at risk of loss to that Empire, and fully aware that the U.S. was not yet in a shooting war with Germany nor were any of America's immediate national interests threatened by Germany, he gave General Marshall this answer:

The people of the Philippines "will excuse failure, but they will not excuse abandonment." He went on to say that while the U.S. was clearly at war in the Pacific and it was a shooting war, and while we were not in a shooting war directly with Germany yet, Ike saw Germany as the more dangerous enemy. He ended their brief meeting with a visionary comment, that:

"This war will be won
by a seaborne invasion of Europe
through France."

Ike could envision, three and a half years before it would ever take place, Allied troops somehow being transported to the French coast and invading Fortress Europe. This required phenomenal abilities of vision as the U.S., at that moment, had no Army, no landing craft and no modern military equipment. And its Navy was badly marred by the attack on Pearl Harbor. As a matter of fact, all Eisenhower had at this moment was **vision and optimism**, two traits that would move him to the top.

After Ike finished, Marshall responded something like, "I agree, do your best."

From that response, Ike assumed he was being sent to the War Plans Department assisting in developing the plans for the eventual invasion of North Africa. After all, the U.S. Army had hundreds of officers superior in rank to Ike from whom Marshall would likely select a commander for the invasion of North Africa.

What Ike didn't know is that Marshall had been monitoring Ike. Marshall knew that this war would eventually ensnare the United States and that it would be vastly different from any previous war. This war would be a modern war, with modern weapons, huge armies, and would cover the entire earth. Those in command would need new skills and talents. Further, this would be a war of allies, and history showed there was nothing more difficult than holding an allied force together in the face of a strong, single national enemy.

Marshall's great genius was acute accuracy in identifying traits in people and matching those traits with jobs. General Marshall kept a small tablet in his breast pocket. On that tablet, he had been recording names of officers he thought would be the leading officers in this next war. Those who would be the young lions with the new and modern skills needed for this very different war. At the top of that list was 'Lt. Col. Eisenhower.'

And with that, Eisenhower was on his way to commanding a large force that would eventually invade North Africa, later Sicily and the boot of Italy, and finally Normandy in France.

Slow Start, then Meteoric Rise
- 1915 - Graduate of West Point Second Lieutenant
- 21 years to get to Lt. Colonel
- 1936 - Lieutenant Colonel
- 1941 – Colonel (temporary grade)
- 1941 - 1 Star General (temporary grade)
- 1942 - 2 Star General (temporary grade)
- 1942 – 3 Star General (temporary grade)
- 1943 - 4 Star General (temporary grade)
- 1944 - 5 Star General (temporary grade)

Note: Even when Ike was a 5 star general (temporary grade), he was officially a permanent Lieutenant Colonel. This would create problems when interacting with British and French Officers of higher permanent rank. Not only was Ike a "hayseed from the Mid-West", he was also just a little Lieutenant Colonel. Ike's Five Star rank was only made permanent in 1962 by an act of Congress after he had left the presidency.

Chapter 3
Ike Now in Charge

Ike's fate would not relegate him to a dead end in War Plans Department, though his skills in planning were a significant factor in General Marshall's mind. As a matter of fact, Ike was eventually named Commanding General, European Theater of Operations and Supreme Commander Allied (Expeditionary) Force of the North African Theater of Operations. This latter command put Ike (the hayseed from Kansas and Texas; the damaged goods that no one wanted leading troops in the field; the second rate, washed-up old man) in command of *all* Allied forces in North Africa. This meant that the man who commanded a nearly non-existent and untested American force was also in command of troops from the great British Empire.

In current thinking, this makes sense, as the US has the larger military. But in 1942, the US had the world's 17th ranked military, rated just below the Romanian military. Yes, you read that correctly, the Romanian military. The US was clearly a second-class power, if that. And the British Empire was at its peak, controlling one-quarter of the earth's surface and fielding troops from India, South Africa, New Zealand, Australia, Canada, Nepal, Burma and myriad other colonies. The British officers viewed themselves as vastly superior in experience and bloodlines to this simple man with a nice smile from the American Dust Bowl. Yet it was Ike, not a British or senior American officer, who was placed in command. Ike's simple yet much-needed skills were beginning to show.

There were many factors making the invasion of North Africa difficult. We will shortly cover the lack of an American military force capable of invading North Africa. Foremost is the fact that North Africa was 5,000 miles across the Atlantic Ocean from American ports. Seaborne invasions are among the most difficult types of military ventures possible. To do it across a vast ocean against an entrenched enemy was unprecedented.

Today with advanced communications, aircraft and navigation, we think little of sending armies around the world. But in 1942, there were no communications satellites. Communication was by radio and no radio could reliably communicate across such an enormous distance. In 1942, no aircraft had adequate range to fly that distance. Moving an invading army across such a sea for such an adventure was a nearly impossible task.

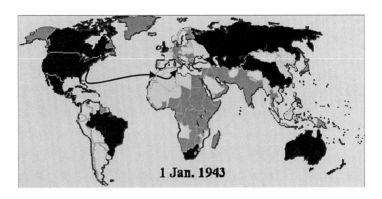

1 Jan. 1943

This is the world at the time of the invasion of North Africa by Allied troops. The nations in black and dark gray are Allied nations. The nations in light gray are Axis nations. 'Axis' was the term used by the alliance of Germany, Italy and Japan during the war.

North Africa was mostly French colonial territory. But with the fall of France to Germany in 1940, all French territory, including her colonies, came under Nazi occupation.

American troops started the war in the Eastern Hemisphere fighting French troops who wanted badly to be part of the Allied forces liberating France.

A Difficult Task: A War without an Army

Beyond the geographical obstacles, the task handed Eisenhower was a seemingly impossible one. The European Axis powers of Germany and Italy had been preparing for war for a decade. The United States had been relishing its neutrality and safety, protected by the great moats of the Atlantic and Pacific. Therefore, most of the US military had been deactivated after World War 1 and had remained relatively deactivated until 1940.

As Recently as 1940, There Was No American Army!

	U.S. 1940	**Germany 1940**
Total military*	130,000	3,000,000
Total tanks	100	4,000
Total aircraft	1,175	6,000

*Army, Navy, Marines and Air Corps

Note: The US military would eventually mobilize around 13,000,000 men and women by war's end. Germany would ultimately mobilize around 18,000,000.

26

At the start of World War II, American tanks were, for the most part, post-World War I quality: small, lightly armored, and under-gunned. The main battle tank fielded by the US at the start of the invasion of North Africa was the General Grant tank. You have probably not heard of the Grant tank as it is long forgotten, and perhaps for good reason. You may think I have mistakenly referenced the wrong Civil War General and that perhaps I should be referring to the General Sherman tank. But the Sherman would not be fielded until after American forces had already waded ashore in North Africa. The General Grant was the main US battle tank in North Africa. The tank boasted a formidable 75mm gun, but the turret had very limited range of fire, essentially straight ahead. Its most useful weapon was the .30 caliber machine gun at the top of the turret. No help at all against an opposing armored vehicle.

American General Grant tank in North Africa. Note the small gun in the mini-turret atop and the 75 mm gun to the left.

To give you an idea of the advantage German armor had over American armor early in war, note the photo below. It is of one of the main German battle tanks used in North Africa at the start of the war, the formidable Tiger I. This 60-ton behemoth carried an extremely effective 88mm (3 inch) cannon that could easily pierce the relatively thin armor of the General Grant (and any subsequent tank developed by the U.S. during the war).

German Tiger Tank captured in North Africa. A 60 ton behemoth with a powerful 88 mm gun. This photo is at the same scale as the Grant tank on the previous page

Poor armor quality wasn't the only shortcoming. The US was also far behind in effective aircraft as well. In 1940, the US had only 1,175 aircraft. And while more modern American aircraft were in the production phase, such as the P-40 Warhawk, and still others were in design, such as the P-38 Lightening, it would be some time before American airmen would be flying them.

At the start of the War, the Germans had 6,000 of the most advanced aircraft in the world: faster and better armed than every aircraft they faced in the early going. Below is the *Messerschmitt* Bf 109, the main fighter aircraft of the German Luftwaffe. Over the course of the war, Germany would manufacture nearly 40,000 Me 109s. It was just one of the many modern aircraft the Luftwaffe would fly.

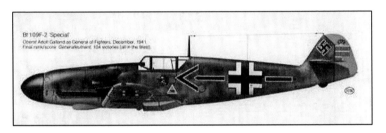

German Messerschmitt Bf 109

American Brewster F2A Buffalo

The most abundant fighter aircraft in the Army Air Corps at the start of the war was the Brewster F2A Buffalo.

Is the American bison, known as the "buffalo", the fastest and most nimble animal on the plains? No, it is a large, slow, lumbering beast that was easy to shoot, much like the fighter plane that carried its name into World War II. Eventually the US would manufacture tens of thousands of aircraft that would rival or exceed anything produced by the enemy. But not yet. Not in 1941. That is not the military Eisenhower started with.

One of Eisenhower's early tasks was to be among many military personnel to travel to American manufacturers throughout the country and work to convince them to convert their consumer manufacturing to the manufacture of military goods. The US Army had to convince companies such as Singer Sewing Machine Company to convert its production lines from manufacturing sewing machines to manufacturing M-1 carbines. They had to convince General Motors to convert their lines from making sedans to Sherman tanks. It was not an easy or quick task, but it was an essential task in the mobilization of America. And Eisenhower had to help accomplish this before he could move troops against enemy forces anywhere in the Eastern Hemisphere.

Ike said the US Army had only one thing in abundance at the start of the war and that was "deficits". Eisenhower started the War with only vision and optimism. These were two valuable qualities that most others did not share.

Chapter 4
Eisenhower on
Enlightened Leadership

Leadership was something Eisenhower had some talent with, yet had to develop more of it quickly. He did have an idea of what would make a good leader. Using criteria he had adopted from General George Marshall, General Eisenhower listed the characteristics of someone he felt would not be fit for promotion.

Characteristics of Someone
Who Will **<u>NOT</u>** Make a Good Leader

- **Self-seeking**
- **Passes the buck**
- **Attempts to do everything himself**
- **Bad manners and discourteous**
- **Great love of the limelight**
- **Treats subordinates as lesser**
- **Pessimistic**

When you read this list of characteristics of those Ike felt were NOT eligible for promotion, you may feel that there are certain officers, famous in their own right, who did fit these characteristics. Gen. George Patton among them. But we will discuss this issue later in the book.

Why Use the Term 'Enlightened Leadership'?

Eisenhower's leadership style was way ahead of its time seventy years ago. His leadership style was so far advanced, that it is still advanced today.

As you read along and see examples of Ike's leadership in action, you may ask yourself, "Where did he learn this?" I think most of it is pretty simple and fundamental. Therefore, I think it is something many people can copy. Ike's leadership is useful because it is so reproducible.

Knowing who would NOT make a good leader is useful. Even more useful is understanding the characteristics of someone who WOULD make a good leader. Eisenhower never put into succinct form what he thought would make a good leader. However in studying Ike's style and examples, a list of leadership traits making an Enlightened Leader stand out.

An Enlightened Leader

- **Exhibits personal integrity**
- **Plans thoroughly and communicates the vision clearly**
- **Selects staff well and backs them completely**
- **Encourages a close, family relationship among staff**
- **Remains optimistic at all times**
- **Deals well with difficult people**
- **Is humble and deflects praise to others**

Ike lived his leadership style every day. And his writings and other's writings on Ike are full of Ike's words on leading people.

Ike on Leading

General Eisenhower and President Eisenhower spoke on leadership many times. His quotes could make a book by themselves and many are interspersed in this book. The three below put his thoughts on leadership rather clearly.

"To be successful, a leader "must be devoted to duty, sincere, fair and cheerful."

"An officer will never make a cohesive unit through embarrassment. Instead, he has to rely on fairness, proper treatment, and leadership through example."

"Hitting a subordinate over the head is not leadership. That's assault."

Chapter 5
An Enlightened Leader
Exhibits Personal Integrity

There were two things that set Ike apart from other officers in World War II. One was his way with people. He had tremendous skills of Diplomacy, mixed with sincere Truthfulness and Integrity. The other was his power of Vision and his skills in Planning.

Diplomacy

As noted earlier, Ike was placed in a difficult command situation. He was an unproven leader with no combat experience who was named Supreme Allied Commander over British officers, who considered themselves superior to Ike in nearly every way. In addition, this position would require Ike to deal directly with the Prime Minister of England, on rare occasion the King of England, on a consistent basis with the British High Command, with the Free French leaders, with leaders of other governments and militaries and with leaders of the U. S. military, senators, members of congress and of course, the President of the United States of America.

One of Eisenhower's chief tasks, and a major reason for his selection, was to hold together an alliance of nations that would inevitably be tested by disparate national interests. And he had to do it knowing that the officers subordinate to him didn't at first believe Ike to be up to the task. His superiors believed Ike had the unique ability to accomplish this.

What Gen. Marshall, the Chief of Staff of the Army, saw in Eisenhower were his diplomatic skills. Such skills came naturally to Ike. He simply liked people. His years serving as Gen. MacArthur's Chief of Staff in the Philippines honed these skills as well. Dealing with Gen. MacArthur and smoothing over difficult situations that MacArthur all too frequently caused was excellent experience for Ike. Ike further polished his skills working with the President of the Philippines and the Philippine military.

Whether you are in an office setting or leading a teetering alliance, diplomatic skills are crucial. Diplomacy can be easily misunderstood. Diplomacy is not avoiding difficult issues. Diplomacy is facing the difficult issues without estranging the other party. To put it another way, "diplomacy is the skill of telling someone to "go to hell!", and have them look forward to the trip. Now that is some skill indeed.

In Stephen Ambrose's book *The Supreme Commander*, Ambrose put it well.

"It was inevitable Eisenhower would have his way. His real achievement was that he had won without alienating the British….He turned them down but only after giving them the opportunity to fully state their views, and

he never let himself be provoked into losing his temper."

Stephen E. Ambrose "The Supreme
Commander"

The Value of Listening

One of the elements of Ike's diplomatic skills was his ability to listen to dissenting opinions. A leader is one who can take people who do not agree with you, yet keep them loyal to the cause. By listening and allowing the British to fully state their views, he demonstrated his respect for their needs and dignity. Of course that didn't mean he would necessarily do what they wanted. Yet he would listen, sincerely listen, to their views. Only after listening fully would he make his decision.

If you as a leader can truly listen to the views of others, especially those who disagree with you, more-than-likely you will retain their loyalty to the team. Dissenters are much likely to remain part of the team even if the decision you make is contrary to their opinion. This is certainly not guaranteed. But if you treat subordinates and dissenters with dignity and sincerely listen to their point of view, they are more likely to feel a part of the team, even if the team is going a direction with which they may not agree. Sincere listening builds loyalty, no matter what. It is a key element in authentic diplomacy.

We don't live in a society that values listening. Observe a typical conversation and there is very listening, the participants essentially take turns 'telling'. That is if they even take turns. Just as often, you will hear the 'listener' begin talking before the speaker has even finished. Sometimes the listener is talking about something totally unrelated to what the speaker related. This isn't a conversation, it is more like verbal sparring.

True listening requires the listener to eliminate judgment and response until the speaker has finished. As soon as you begin to form a response: you have stopped listening. As soon as you begin to agree or disagree, you have stopped listening. If you have start to mentally criticize or judge, or evaluate by any standard, you have stopped listening.

Listening, sincere listening, requires several things. First, for the speaker to trust you are listening, it is essential to give the listener your complete concentration. Second, you should avoid performing other tasks while listening (or partially listening). While many people are able to multi-task, it still communicates to the listener that the speaker or what the speaker is saying is not important. Concentrating on the speaker with limited interruptions gives you the best chance to earn the speaker's respect.

Truthfulness and Integrity

A leadership trait that often surprises people is the trait of integrity. Many people can recite a litany of examples of leaders who clearly lacked integrity, yet still led. An important question is always, "How long did they lead and how did it all end up?" Another question is, "Was that leadership, which implies people want to follow, or was that 'dictatorship', which forces people to follow?" Often, leaders of low integrity can lead for a while, yet the lack of integrity eventually catches up to them and derails them.

Certainly there are different leadership styles. But I am looking to the highest ideal of leadership; namely, those traits that comprise "enlightened" leadership.

There is no way around it; Ike was a hayseed from the Midwest. He was constantly dealing with British blue bloods who, like I have said, saw themselves as Ike's superior in nearly every way. Somehow Ike slowly won them over during his command. It is very worthwhile to see the quotes of his former subordinates from the British military and learn what it was that allowed them to build trust in Ike.

One of Ike's direct subordinates was First Sea Lord, Sir Andrew B. Cunningham, Royal Navy, Naval Chief of Staff. This high-ranking British naval officer was in charge of a significant part of the world's largest and most powerful navy. Yet he reported to Eisenhower and, at first, didn't think much of him. Yet after the war he wrote,

> *"He struck me as being completely sincere, straightforward and very modest...*
>
> *It was not long before I realized him as the really great man he is - forceful, able, direct and far-seeing..."*
>
> First Sea Lord, Sir Andrew B. Cunningham
> Royal Navy, Naval Chief of Staff

At another time, Lord Cunningham wrote,

"It was not long before we discovered that our Commander was a man of outstanding integrity."

But the most telling quote of all comes from one of Eisenhower's most difficult subordinates. Frankly, British Field Marshall Bernard Montgomery was nearly everyone's most difficult subordinate. His own Prime Minister, Winston Churchill once called Montgomery "The most irritating man in the universe." Yet, after the war, Montgomery wrote about Eisenhower,

> *"...his real strength lies in his human qualities...He has the power of drawing the hearts of men towards him as a magnet attracts bits of metal. He merely has to smile at you, and you trust him at once. He is the very incarnation of sincerity."*

"The very incarnation of sincerity." Not a comment you hear often in the corporate world. Not a comment you hear often from military officers, especially those who were once strongly opposed to the man being complemented. Sincerity is what eventually allowed the British leaders to trust Eisenhower. They knew that Eisenhower was not simply a mouthpiece for American military, economic, or political interests. Eisenhower was there to truly and sincerely represent all allied parties and keep them satisfied and unified. He was there to win the war. Nothing more, nothing less.

Truthfulness Brings the End to Hostilities

One of the greatest examples of Eisenhower's truthfulness bringing immediate, concrete results occurred during the campaign in North Africa. It is important to know the French military leaders in North Africa were in a horrible position. France had been defeated by Germany in very short order early in the war. With the defeat and occupation of France, Germany inherited all of France's colonies around the world, including those vast territories in North Africa.

When the Allies invaded North Africa to wrestle it away from the Nazis, the French military and civilian government in North Africa were caught between a rock and a hard place. While most soldiers and citizens in Africa desperately preferred to be a part of the alliance of nations attacking Germany, their families were at home in France under the occupation of Nazi forces. The lives of the families of the soldiers defending the shores of North Africa from invasion were literally at stake.

The French authorities in North Africa had to somehow seek surrender in order to join the Allies, yet not surrender too easily and anger their Nazi occupiers. This was an extraordinarily difficult time for the French. And many lives were lost, on both sides, as the French put up a limited defense of their African colonies.

As the military forces in French West Africa were preparing for surrender, the British, American and French leaders met for the surrender conference in the office of the Governor General of French West Africa, Pierre Boisson. Eisenhower was among the officers present. As the meeting progressed, latent hostilities stemming from hundreds of years of conflict between the British and French erupted. The British and French officers, facing each other across the conference table in Boisson's office, began a screaming match. Among the various issues being argued at full voice, the French were demanding concessions that Eisenhower was powerless to address. He could only present the surrender agreement that had been hammered out in London and Washington, DC. He could not change it.

Eisenhower was disgusted with the behavior of both sides. Realizing they were accomplishing nothing in this atmosphere, he motioned to Governor General Boisson to come with him to a quieter corner of the office near Boisson's desk. He said to Boisson, *"It'll take weeks to straighten this out with the leaders. If you will simply sign the surrender agreement, I will do everything I can as a soldier to make sure that the general arrangements are carried out. The spirit of our agreement will never be violated."*

Boisson looked at Eisenhower. He looked at the arguing officers at the conference table, nearly coming to blows. Then he looked back at the face of Eisenhower. He realized Ike was conceding nothing in writing. All Ike was offering to the French was an unwritten promise. There was nothing concrete the French could refer back to and demand satisfaction on if Ike failed to follow through. Ike was essentially asking this former adversary and complete stranger to "trust him."

Boisson then said,

> *"I have found and all other French leaders tell me that you will not lie or evade in any dealings with us, even when it appears you could easily do so."*

With that, Governor General Boisson took the surrender agreement, sat at his desk, and signed it. Based solely on trust in Ike's sterling reputation of integrity, the hostilities in French West Africa ended. How many thousands of lives were saved by Ike's honesty and integrity?

A good question to ask your self as a leader is "Am I honest? Am I trustworthy? Do I really have the integrity that would prompt an adversary or a co-worker to trust me to this degree? If your answer is 'yes', test your self. Ask others in some fashion if you are trustworthy. Watch your own behavior and observe the real level of your integrity.

On the other hand, if your answer is no, ask yourself if you can afford to continue that way. Then begin to work on living in greater integrity. The payoff will be far more than you could ever imagine.

Keep in mind, you don't have to be trustworthy or honest. Each person chooses how to live life. Just remember, there are consequences for every action. If you are not trustworthy, those who work for you, those who you work for, will not trust you. It is that simple.

The difficulty is, to be considered trustworthy, you have to be trustworthy all the time. Not most of the time. It takes a long time to build trust, but only a moment to destroy it. And once destroyed, it takes forever to rebuild.

Integrity means doing the right thing...even when no one is watching. Integrity is a power. Live in integrity, and you will have great power.

PRACTICAL IDEAS ON PERSONAL INTEGRITY

Think of someone you consider trustworthy.
1. Why do you consider that person trustworthy?
2. Have you seen that person do what is right, even when it would be easier to take a shortcut?
3. Has any person ever let you down by not being trustworthy?
4. How long did it take for that person to weaken or destroy your trust?
5. How long did it take for you to have trust in that person again (if ever)?

Ask yourself:
1. Am I trustworthy?
2. If I say I am going to do something, do I follow through?
3. Do I return phone messages I promise to return?
4. Do I follow through on obligations or do I sometimes conveniently ignore them?
5. If a clerk gives me too much change, do I give it back?
6. Am I honest with others at all times?

Ask yourself this vital question: What is my highest aspiration?
1. Wealth
2. Fame
3. Knowledge
4. Popularity
5. Integrity

If your answer is other than 'integrity', be aware of the consequences. When push comes to shove, and integrity is not your highest aspiration, a choice must be made. What will you chose?*

* *adapted from the works of L. Murphy Smith, Professor of Accounting at Texas A&M University*

Chapter 6
An Enlightened Leader Plans Thoroughly, Communicates Vision Well

You probably take part in some kind of planning process in your organization. It is certainly common. Yet often, the strategy and plans are retained at the top level like a corporate secret. The plans, once determined, are often not shared with the people on the front lines. And these are the very people who must carry out the plans.

Even more common, plans are made without any real vision of what the organization is attempting to accomplish. The power of a vision cannot be overstated. Vision is often what can push an organization further than ever before. Plans without vision are not useless, they may simply keep you busy while running in place.

And perhaps, most common of all, where there is a vision, the leader of the organization is often unable to communicate it clearly and believably to a staff. Visionary leadership is a game changer. If you, as a leader, can develop a meaningful, shared vision among your people, half of your work in achieving it is already done.

> *"We succeed only as we identify in life, or in war, or in anything else, a single overriding objective, and make all other considerations bend to that one objective."*
>
> Gen. Dwight D. Eisenhower

Remember what Eisenhower said to General Marshall in there first meeting?

"This war will be won by a seaborne invasion of Europe through France."

This vision was something that Ike had to share, over and over again, with his subordinates. As a matter of fact, he had to share it, and sell it, over and over again to his superiors. Ike never varied from this original plan, though nearly everyone else above him did. Roosevelt, Churchill, De Gaulle, and even Soviet Marshall Stalin tried at various times to get Eisenhower to change the invasion plans or timing. Ike was steadfast in his direction. He must have doubted himself on occasion, but publicly he never waivered. It is not that he was stubborn. Ike was clear. There is a difference.

"History has proved that nothing is more difficult in war than to adhere to a single strategic plan."

Eisenhower, Crusade in Europe

Along with vision goes the task of planning. Ike, the master planner, was also acutely aware of the shortcomings of planning. He was quoted as saying:

"Going into battle without a plan is foolhardy. But as soon as the shooting starts, the plan is useless."

47

Another time he said,

"In preparing for battle I have always found that plans are useless, but planning is indispensable."

By the time the great "seaborne invasion of Europe through France" was to take place in June of 1944, the tide of the war had clearly changed. The Nazis no longer had superior aircraft and a superior military. While their tanks would continue to be superior in weapons and armor than Allied tanks, Allied tanks were produced in such quantity, they simply outnumbered the enemy tanks.

The Tide Changes by D-Day

Allies	1940	June 6, 1944
Total soldiers	140,000	2,900,000
Total tanks	100	5,000
Total aircraft	1,175	16,000
Naval craft		6,000

The figures on the left represent the entire U.S. military in 1940, the figures on the right are simply for the invasion of Normandy; an enormous change from pre-war numbers.

Normandy, 1944

As you look at this photo of the beachhead at Normandy, taken some time after D-Day, you begin to grasp the enormity of this invasion. Ships stretch for as far as the eye could see. Soldiers, vehicles and materiel crowded the beach which just a short time before had been littered with the debris of war.

On the day of the invasion, the Allies were able to get 156,000 troops onto the Continent of Europe. Within the next week, more than 1,000,000 men would cross these beaches and bring the battle to the enemy.

Putting this into context can help. Milwaukee, Wisconsin is a metropolitan area of roughly one million residents. What the Allies accomplished in this invasion was the equivalent of picking up the entire population of

Milwaukee, Wisconsin; every man, woman, and child; every vehicle, every piece of clothing, and all the pots and pans, and typewriters; add to that tanks, and artillery and ammunition, and enough food to feed a million young, hungry men, and put this all onto ships, and deliver it all across Lake Michigan and deposit everything on the shores from Saint Joseph, Michigan to Muskegon, Michigan…in a week …with somebody shooting at them.

It was an undertaking of epic proportions.

Eisenhower and the Allies had turned England into a massive aircraft carrier off the coast of Europe. The Island was overflowing with three million soldiers, sailors and airmen planning and training for the great invasion. The training and planning started in earnest eight months before D-Day. Eight months of planning and training, training and planning, planning and training. You get the idea. The level of training and planning was so high, that men in the first waves of the invasion had reviewed sand tables, maps and aerial photos of the area where they would land. They knew what they would see when they got there and what their immediate task was.

Yet, just as Eisenhower said, *"Going into battle without a plan is foolhardy. But as soon as the shooting starts, the plan is useless."*

Within one hour of the start of the great invasion, even after eight months of planning and training, the plan was useless.

The first troops to invade France were the airborne troops, the American 82nd and 101st Airborne Divisions and the British 6th Airborne Division. These men, nearly thirty thousand in total, left the air bases in England late on the night of June 5th. 1944. Travelling in over one thousand transports and gliders, these men would cross the English Channel in the dark of night. By mid-night, they were crossing the English Channel. Within an hour from their aircraft rendezvous they would be crossing the French coast; and the plan would already be useless.

In this modern day, pilots navigate using GPS systems and know to the yard where they are at any given moment. In 1944, pilots navigated by "dead reckoning". This meant they used a compass heading, gauged wind speed for drift, and used a watch to determine how long they were following each compass heading.

The American Airborne divisions had an especially challenging task. Their flight plan took them first south along the French coast paralleling Normandy, then a hard left to cross into French airspace at the end of the Cotentin Peninsula, then a hard left again to work their way back up the French coast flanking the landing beaches. This task was made all the more difficult because it was being flown at night.

To ratchet up the level of difficulty even further, the weather on the night of June 5th, 1944 was horrid. A powerful storm had worked over the British Isles and the Normandy coast. The skies in the flight path were cloudy and the winds were powerful. Eisenhower had seriously contemplated calling off the invasion as the weather was so grossly unfavorable for a successful Allied landing. All this made navigating by dead reckoning an extreme challenge.

Oh, but there was one more thing. The pilots ferrying the airborne troops into France were cargo pilots. These men had never flown into anti-aircraft fire before. Had they been seasoned bomber pilots, they would have known that when you encounter anti-aircraft fire, you fly directly through it. The reason was simple; when navigating by dead reckoning, deviating from your course to avoid anti-aircraft fire meant you were now flying off course.

The original airborne invasion plan called for the British and two American Airborne divisions to land in three distinct areas. Due to the more direct British flight path, the British troops were able to land relatively close to their intended targets. Instead of landing in their two distinct landing areas, the unfortunate American divisions landed over an eighty kilometer swath of French countryside. Instead of 30,000 allied troops being in those three distinct areas, there were Allied Airborne troops all around the Normandy coast.

If a "stick" or "unit" landed close to their intended target, they were lucky. The vast majority of soldiers hit the ground, looked for the landmarks they had so carefully studied in their invasion training, and found they could recognize nothing. Where there should be a church steeple, there would be a hill or woods instead. Most were nowhere near where they were supposed to be. *"... as soon as the shooting starts, the plan is useless."*

But you know what? Here's the amazing thing. It didn't matter. Due to the quality training, these men knew that if the task they were trained to do was no longer feasible, they would try something else. They had been trained in the overall *vision* of their leader...the destruction of Nazism, and the basic strategy of the airborne assault: one, to protect the bridges from destruction; two, to stop reinforcements from making it to the Normandy beachhead; and three, to cut enemy communications from the coast.

In the confusion of the mis-landings, field leaders patched together mixed units, made up of men who had never seen each other or worked together before, and set out to accomplish the three basic tasks: hold the bridges, stop reinforcements, and cut communications. And they did it well.

Oddly, many historians contend that by having airborne troops so widely dispersed, the Allied invasion plan was actually aided. Reports of paratroopers landing in so many sectors caused the German High Command to initially estimate the airborne drop at 120,000 troops, not the 30,000 that actually landed. This estimate slowed the High Command's decision-making and forced them to delay counter-attacks. They didn't know where to send their counter-attack. That delay allowed the airborne troops to solidify their positions in the French countryside and the seaborne troops to gain a foothold on the beaches.

Strategically Necessary versus Strategically Desirable

In any organization, the demands are limitless but the resources are often very limited. This is true in business, this is true in battle. Eisenhower knew that the demands on his troops, vehicles, tanks and supplies were huge. The United States was fighting a two front war in the Pacific and Europe, and Eisenhower was fighting a broad front war ranging from Holland to Italy. This war involved millions of men, hundreds of thousands of vehicles, aircraft and ships, and field commanders who needed more of everything.

Without clear prioritization, the resources could be squandered attempting to meet the needs of everyone a little bit rather than meeting the most important needs well.

One of Eisenhower's great concepts was to determine what was 1) Strategically Necessary and what was 2) Strategically Desirable. Once you determine what is Strategically Necessary, then "maximum resources" should be allocated to those areas.

What about the areas that are Strategically Desirable? Allocate "minimal resources" to those areas.

Further, Eisenhower said that the distinction should be rigidly observed, meaning, you should not cave in to persuasive arguments or hotheaded supervisors who demanded more. Stay true to the designation of what is Strategically Necessary, and don't waiver.

During one of my management classes at Gonzaga University, we were studying time management. The professor reached under his desk during this discussion and lifted a glass three-gallon mayonnaise jar and placed it on top of the desk. Then he opened a drawer and pulled out three large, smoothly rounded river rocks. He gently placed the river rocks into the glass jar. The three rocks were so large they took up all the space in the jar, the tip of the top rock protruding slightly above the rim.

Then he looked at the expectant class and asked, "Can I fit any more into the jar?" One student, mirroring my thoughts said, "No, it's full."

The professor then reached into another drawer and took out a small bucket of gravel and slowly poured it into the jar until it reached the top. He smoothed it off with his hand and asked, "Now, can I fit any more into this jar?" Half the class said "No". The other half figured the good professor had something up his sleeve and responded "Yes".

He opened another drawer and pulled out a small bucket of fine sand. He gently poured the sand into the jar, topping it off again. "OK, now can I fit more into the jar?" We were all getting it by now and said, "Yes, Professor, somehow you are going to."

And of course he did, this time he reached below the desk and lifted a big glass of water, pouring water over the sand, gravel and rocks until it came level with the lip of the jar.

Then he asked, "What have I just taught you about time management?"

A student raised her hand and guessed, "You can always fit more in?"

"No", said the professor, "You missed my point completely. The three big rocks are my three biggest priorities. If I didn't identify them and put them in first, I would never be able to shove them in past the sand and gravel. But since I put them in first, I can always fit the items of lesser importance (the sand and gravel) around the highest priorities.

This is an example of identifying what is Strategically Necessary and what is Strategically Desirable. If you find your "big rocks" and put your resources of time, materials and money behind them, you are very likely to achieve them. And the funny thing is, all the not so important stuff…the Strategically Desirable stuff…seems to get taken care of too.

Differentiate between:

Strategically Necessary
Maximum resources should be allocated to Strategically Necessary

Strategically Desirable
Minimal resources should be allocated to Strategically Desirable

The distinction should be "rigidly" observed

Planning at the Strategic Level
1. Remain committed to the Vision
2. Make all other objectives "bend" to that Vision

Another of Eisenhower's concepts was the importance of staying true to a Vision, while never becoming rigid at the tactical level.

Once a vision is created, Eisenhower said to make all other objectives "bend" to that vision.

Ike's vision was not the defeat of Germany. I suspect his German background gave him some distant empathy for the people. Ike's vision was for the "destruction of Nazism". Ike hated Nazism and wanted to see it stamped out and removed from the earth. This was his vision.

His lesser vision was that "this war will be won by a seaborne invasion of Europe through France."

Planning at the Tactical Level

While the vision is key and must be rigidly observed, the way to get there needs to be flexible. Eisenhower cautioned his officers to never let their minds become set or rigid. The reason for this mental agility is because the situation on the ground or in the marketplace can never be truly planned. There are too many possibilities that can arise that planners can't even predict.

In planning, it is very helpful to create situations that give you several alternatives. Getting into a situation without alternatives can lead to success, but it can also lead to unmitigated disaster.

Remaining flexible in the market or battlefield is essential. By remaining flexible, you are in a more creative space. As new and unexpected situations arise, your mental agility often leads to unexpected and successful responses.

Mental agility
1. Never let your mind become set or rigid
2. Create situations that give you several alternatives
3. Remain flexible always

If it Achieves the Vision but Doesn't Meet the Plan, Ignore the Plan!

As noted earlier, Ike had two great talents, and one of them was his talent in planning. As the war changed and progressed, the overall plans changed and progressed. As Allied units rushed across Europe and began their push into Germany, the main battle plans called for a broad front with troops putting pressure on the Germans in many places along the battle line. However, the planners saw that there were areas that were better places to fight a modern tank war and there were lesser places. In that vein, the main British Army Group led by Field Marshall Montgomery was pushing along the northern part of the front at Dusseldorf and Cologne. The main US Army Group led by General Omar Bradley was farther to the south between Bingen and Strasbourg. A French lead army was farther south in the very difficult terrain of the Vosges Mountains.

Between Montgomery's Army and Bradley's Army was a part of the front that the planners considered very minor and less important. It was hilly with very irregular terrain and frankly, not a very good place to fight a war. So they assigned few troops to this area.

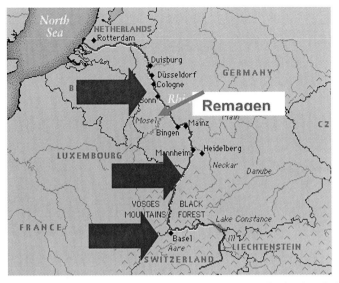

The Remagen Bridge, Remagen, Germany. Only bridge left over the Rhine.

The Remagen Bridge didn't fit any plan. So? Ignore the plan!

In March of 1945, Allied troops had pushed the enemy to the perennial defensive protection of Germany; the Rhine River. After achieving victory after the month long Battle of the Bulge, Allied troops finally pierced the German border and advanced into Germany west of the Rhine. But by March, they hit another road block and could not break through. The Rhine River, which had protected the German tribes from the Roman invaders 2,000 years earlier, was now holding back the massive Allied advance.

Each time Allied troops would reach the Rhine, the Germans would destroy any existing bridges near the point of advance. To this point, the Germans had to use the bridges to supply German troops still fighting west of the Rhine. But now the defenders were using the bridges to withdraw the Wehrmacht troops back into the heartland of Germany as the Western Front continued to collapse.

The Allied armies had fabulous engineers and ingenious bridging equipment which certainly could span the Rhine. But the winter of 1944-45 was one of the worst Europe had experienced in a century. As a result, the Rhine was fed by more rain and snow than usual and was much wider and faster flowing than during a normal spring run-off. Just as importantly, very accurate German artillery situated on the far side of the river would wipe out army engineers each time they attempted to build a pontoon bridge. Commanders griped about the engineers' inability to complete a bridge, but were given the same response over and over: "Sir, you can't build a bridge when they're dropping bombs on your head."

The result was that Allied troops were again at a standstill. Without a standing bridge to establish a bridgehead on the far side of the Rhine, they were stuck. The war had come to a standoff again.

On March 7th, a patrol travelling along a road on the west side of the Rhine reached a bluff across the river from Remagen, Germany. What they saw shocked them. A bridge. A standing bridge. A complete, undamaged, span across the river. Somehow Allied pilots had failed to note this standing bridge.

These troops immediately radioed their commander to tell him of the bridge. Their commander was fully aware of the Battle Plan and the Battle Plan called for the vast majority of their millions of troops to push far to the north or far to the south. He told his men to hold while he contacted his superior, but in the meantime he sent some more troops to support this patrol.

On March 7th, an American patrol arrived at the bridge

This commander radioed his superior who essentially said, "Well, that's not a big deal, the planners are calling for the advances to be to the north and south." But just to be sure, he called General Omar Bradley. Bradley was excited about finally finding a bridge and he immediately called his boss and old buddy, Ike.

Ike had been terribly frustrated by this standoff. When he got the call from General Bradley informing him of a standing bridge in the middle of nowhere, his staff reported Ike "Whooped like a teenager" and said "Brad, get as many troops across that bridge as fast as you can!"

*"In preparing for battle I have always
found that plans are useless, but planning
is indispensable."*

Eisenhower knew that the 'plan' wasn't important. The
'vision' and 'overall strategy' were important. When a
tactic becomes a controlling point, especially when current
information tells you that the tactic isn't working or that
another tactic will bring you better results, it is often best to
ignore the "plan" and try the a new tactic.

Bradley shifted his troops to the north to take advantage
of this breech. The unit that originally discovered the intact
bridge secured it after a tough fight. The Germans tried to
detonate the explosives that had been pre-placed
throughout the bridge, but the explosives failed to detonate.
They then attempted to use their own artillery and air
power to destroy the bridge, but the bridge was well built
and took the hits without failing. Between March 7th when
the bridge was found and March 17th, when the Germans
finally succeeded in destroying the bridge, Bradley was
able to push four divisions, more than 50,000 men, across
the bridge. This gave the Americans the much-needed
bridgehead, allowing the engineers enough calm to build a
series of pontoon bridges across the mighty Rhine, thus
permitting a nearly endless flow of men and equipment into
the heart of the Third Reich. The war would be over in less
than fifty days. Nazism would be destroyed within two
months.

The key lesson here is flexibility and mental agility. No matter how good the plan, it must be flexible. It is best if there is a process in the plan to allow for modifications to be made as the plan is carried out.

PRACTICAL IDEAS ON
PLANNING AND COMMUNICATING

STRATEGIC NECESSITY

As mentioned earlier, it is important to discern for your organization what is Necessary for the Achievement of the vision and what is only Desirable.

When developing or reviewing strategy, determine on each topic whether the item is Necessary or Desirable. If you end up with a lot of Necessary items, you have been too lenient on the definition of Necessary. Go back and try again. Strategically Necessary items should be limited to three to six items.

<u>Strategically Necessary</u>

Maximum resources should be allocated to Strategically Necessary

<u>Strategically Desirable</u>

Minimal resources should be allocated to Strategically Desirable

<u>Neither of the Above</u>

These would be items that don't rise even to the level of Desirable. These would be the "Nice to Have" items, or issues of regulatory compliance.

EISENHOWER PRIORITIZATION METHOD

Importance

	IMPORTANT	UNIMPORTANT
URGENT	**1** Important and Urgent	**2** Not Important but Urgent
NOT URGENT	**3** Important but not Urgent	**4** Neither Important nor Urgent

Urgency

A key to prioritizing on a daily basis or in developing strategy is to understand priorities. This little grid can be a helpful item. It is something many effective people use on a daily basis.

1: Important and Urgent. This is clearly a top priority. Put your utmost attention and energy on this to get it done soon and well.

2: Unimportant but Urgent. This is usually some deadline that is approaching for something not tactically or strategically important, yet it has to be done. Make sure to carve out time to get it done on time. These are usually activities that have few positive implications but can have distinctive negative consequences. Most regulatory compliance or tax issues fit into this category.

3: Important but not Urgent. You have some time to work on this and it is tactically or strategically important. Don't wait until the last minute. Make sure to plan adequate time to complete it before it becomes urgent. This is how you can get out of the "putting out fires" trap.

4: Unimportant and Not Urgent. The majority of day-to-day activities fall into this category. Fit these in when possible and work hard to avoid them falling into category 2 due to procrastination. Consider dropping these off your To-Do List.

This grid can be helpful in prioritizing team goals and duties as well as those of individuals. If you have a colleague or employee who is having difficulty accomplishing tasks, encourage them to use this grid. This grid will help you adjust some tasks, remove some priorities entirely, and make sure that you both agree on what falls into the urgent/important quadrant.

Chapter 7
An Enlightened Leader
Selects Staff Well and
Backs Them Completely

"True delegation implies the courage and readiness to back up a subordinate to the full..."

A leader can lead by force, or a leader can lead by persuasion. Sometimes a leader has to move between the two, but force usually burns out sooner and becomes less effective over time while leading by persuasion tends to become self-perpetuating. Ike said:

> *"I would rather try to persuade a man to go along, because once I have persuaded him he will stick. If I scare him, he will stay just as long as he is scared, and then he is gone."*

Another time he commented:

> *"The idea is to get people to working together, not only because you tell them to do so...but because they instinctively want to do it for you."*

In order to lead successfully by persuasion, you first need the right people in the right positions. As noted earlier, this was a key talent of Gen. Marshall, who identified Eisenhower's talents and put him in the right position.

Peter Drucker, the business guru spoke of this when he said,

"Your business's greatest asset is not your people. Your business's greatest asset is the 'right' people."

Ike took time to learn how to identify and use the right people. He had to assist in building an effective command structure and headquarters team. He had to learn how and when to promote and relieve commanders in the field. None of this came easy to him. And his difficulty in learning this important lesson undoubtedly cost lives.

During the early part of the North Africa campaign, Ike relied heavily on Gen. Freidenhall, whose reputation as a soldier and commander was sterling. Yet when Ike learned that Friedenhall was overly cautious, he didn't replace him. Even when Ike learned that Freidenhall had hollowed an underground cave system for his headquarters in North Africa where he and his staff would be safe while his soldiers were in harm's way, Ike scolded him, but didn't replace him. This he would eventually do, but historians say he learned this lesson much too slowly.

Once he did learn this lesson, he became much more effective.

Ike's natural inclination was to draw out the creative talents of people. The reason was, his organization was so large he was simply unable to make or even review all the mid-level decisions. Eisenhower believed that assistants must solve their own problems and tell their leader later what they had done.

In today's terms, we would say he "empowered" his staff.

Ike's role in tactical arrangements was limited.
1. He set the general policy
2. But day-to-day operations were in the hands of subordinates.

"He sometimes had to nod in general agreement without knowing the details."

Here was his general process of empowerment:

1. He gave staff a task
2. He avoided looking over their shoulder
3. He resisted guiding them to a solution
4. If well done, he was quick to give them credit
5. If failure, he took the blame himself

Ike selected staff carefully. He found people with special talents and strengths. Had he attempted to micro-manage his staff he would have exhausted himself, he would have thwarted their innovation and self-motivation, and his staff would have been disenchanted by their inability to fully exhibit their talents.

According to Eisenhower, a leader should not impose his or her own will, but through persuasion and cooperation, draw on the talents of his or her staff.

Montgomery's Style Versus Eisenhower's Style

One of Ike's most difficult and important employees was the popular British Field Marshall, Bernard Law Montgomery, the Hero of El Alamein, a decisive battle in North Africa. Montgomery was very popular among the British people. England had been battered around by the Nazis since 1940. Montgomery led the British to its first significant victory over Axis forces during the Battle of El Alamein in Egypt in 1942 after two long years of war. He was also popular among the soldiers he led. However, Monty was not popular among his fellow British officers. And it is safe to say he was despised by his American counterparts.

Monty

Ike

As mentioned before, even his own boss, Prime Minister Winston Churchill, who would never relieve Monty due to his popularity, called him, "The most irritating man in the universe."

Eisenhower found him to be an extremely difficult subordinate to work with. Ike would have preferred to have relieved Monty and replace him with a more cooperative and aggressive General, one who would attack without the elaborate plans and build-up Montgomery always required.

There are many different leadership styles. The difference in style between Monty and Ike is very telling. Both men were talented in and rightfully proud of their planning skills.

To develop a battle plan, Monty would sequester himself in his field trailer, the very trailer he had 'liberated'  from the German Desert Fox, General Rommel, during the Allied victory in North Africa. Monty would stay in his trailer for days drawing up an elaborate battle plan by himself. When completed, he would give the plan to his aid, order copies to be made, and have the aid deliver the plan to his commanders in the field. It was a top-down planning process. There was little or no two-way communication from the field commanders to the Field

Marshall on how the plan could be improved or how the plan might not reflect the battlefield realities. Monty would simply expect the men to carry out his plan. Fortunately, he was a talented planner and tactician and had much battlefield success (and a few whopping failures) during the war.

Eisenhower's process was entirely different. He would gather his team, including planners, headquarters staff and field commanders, into a big room. Ike would sit in his chair with his leg draped over the armrest. He would have a perpetual cup of coffee in one hand and cigarette in the other. Then he and the planning team would discuss the situation and the options.

In this method, many points of view from many experienced and intelligent minds were tapped for their ideas, cautions, innovations, and battlefield realities that Ike could never engender by himself. The ideas would be discussed, questioned, attacked, supported and discussed some more. This didn't guarantee a good decision. But it did increase the chances that issues and ideas were not missed.

Ike thought respectful dissent was essential to the making of a team. He didn't need 'yes men'. He needed competent people who could tell others when their ideas were good or bad. Eisenhower once said,

"Never confuse honest dissent with disloyal subversion."

Allowing dissent is frightening for many leaders. It can lead to unknowns. Dissenters are often cruelly cast as enemies.

A key element in building a true team is to let others have their say. According to the book "Five Dysfunctions of a Team" by Patrick Lencioni, a team cannot be created without something he identifies as "unfiltered criticism". Unfiltered criticism is the right of each team member to state his or her views even if those views do not conform with the ideas of the leader or the rest of the team.

If team members are allowed to truly state their dissent, the team is strengthened by alternative points of view, and the dissenting team member is implicitly or explicitly told by the team that their viewpoint matters. This creates loyalty even if the dissenter's viewpoint is not accepted as the team's.

On the other hand, if dissent is quashed, dissent doesn't go away, it becomes hidden. It becomes an undercurrent instead of out in the open. Quashing dissent simply causes a dissenter to publicly accept a decision while privately not supporting the decision. As a result, dissenters will often work subversively to undermine the efforts of the team or work through back channels to manipulate the team into a different direction. This is when an environment becomes political. Groups that are political work for personal gain versus collective results.

Take the Blame for Subordinates' Mistakes

Ike once joked,

"Leadership consists of nothing but taking responsibility for everything that goes wrong and giving your subordinates credit for everything that goes well."

As a leader, Ike was often willing to take the blame for subordinates' mistakes. As part of empowering his subordinates, Ike needed them to make decisions on their own. These were decisions that may or may not have been what Eisenhower would have made. Freedom to fail is key to empowerment.

If a subordinate is instructed to make decisions on his own, then punished if a mistake is made, the subordinate will soon learn there is no real advantage to making decisions on his own. The subordinate may act like he is making decisions or he may simply defer decisions back to his superior.

The greatest way to ensure your staff never makes a mistake is to punish them every time they fail. Unfortunately that also removes all staff drive and self-motivation.

Take blame for subordinates' mistakes so that they are free to make decisions without fear.

Ike knew a leader has to be willing to take the blame for subordinates' mistakes. In this way, subordinates become free to make decisions without fear. If they are free to make decisions without fear, they will learn from their mistakes and get better at their jobs. If, however, they don't demonstrate an ability to learn and instead continue to make the same mistake or develop new and creative mistakes, then they have demonstrated they are the wrong person for that position or for your company.

Not Failure but Feedback

Keep in mind, a mistake, when looked at properly, does not have to represent failure, but feedback. If something goes poorly, it is feedback that something was wrong with what you just did. Either the idea was unsound, or its delivery was poor, or something else wasn't right. But it need not be treated as failure.

I think an old corporate legend is a good metaphor for this concept. According to the legend, in the 1970s, IBM hired a young new executive-in-training, a fresh Business School graduate. After a bit of time, the young executive had an idea he wanted to put into practice. His supervisor thought it would be good to let him run with it. As the project progressed, it was clear the project was not going well. As a matter of fact, this project might have been deemed an abject failure. Apparently, according to the legend, IBM lost $250,000 on this debacle. In 1970's dollars, that was very big money.

When the extent of the failure was evident, the young exec was summoned to his boss's office. Dejectedly, the young man entered the office and took a seat across the desk from his boss. Before any words were exchanged, the young man slipped a sheet of paper across the desk and let it rest in front of his boss. The boss glanced at it and asked, "What's that?" The young man stammered, "It's, it's my resignation. You called me in to fire me, didn't you?" The boss had a surprised look on his face and responded, "Fire you. Why would I fire you? We just spent $250,000 dollars on your education!"

If a staffer doesn't seem to learn from the feedback from mistakes, the leader must be aware of that too. A leader needs discernment in this area. If a leader is regularly getting feedback that someone is not working out, the feedback may be that the staff member is the wrong person for that position. As we will see in the chapter entitled *Dealing Well with Difficult People,* Eisenhower declared we must be decisive in removing people who don't work out.

A good leader will always learn from feedback. Sometimes he learns how to do something better next time; sometimes he learns that a person is not right for the position or the organization.

Accountability

While this section is entitled *An Enlightened Leader Selects Staff Well and Back Them Completely*, Ike didn't *always* back his staff completely. He was very practical. If the feedback he received indicated a commander was the wrong one for a position, Ike would eventually, or sometimes quickly, remove the commander from that position. He obviously had to replace many people. He even fired his most effective commander Gen. George Patton, not once but twice, because Patton's political blunders were so damaging to morale and the Allied cause as to reduce his ability to command.

On the other hand, a great example of Ike's willingness to take the blame for failure revolved around the massive Invasion of Normandy, D-Day. Today, we look back and see the Allied success in breaching Fortress Europe. It seems like it was foregone conclusion that the Allies would succeed in Normandy. With the luxury of hindsight, success seemed guaranteed. However, at the time, the invasion was by no means a guaranteed success. An invasion by sea of a fortified coast is one of the most difficult and dangerous military actions possible. At the time of the invasion, Army planners gave Allied forces only a 50-50 chance of success. Those are not great odds.

To complicate matters, the original date for the invasion, June 5th, had to be delayed. The weather leading up to and on June 5, 1944 was abominable. Rain was coming down so hard and the winds over the Channel and on the invasion beaches were so strong, that a seaborne and airborne invasion were out of the question.

This created a great tactical problem. Thousands of ships had already been loaded with over 100,000 Allied troops. These ships were waiting in harbors all around Great Britain for the order to commence sailing toward the attack.

Some convoys had already set sail and if the invasion were further delayed they would have to be recalled, not an easy task under radio silence. Yet the storm brought gale force winds whipping the English Channel to sixteen-foot waves and a cloud cover so thick and menacing that Allied air effectiveness would be completely nullified.

After an agonizing day, Eisenhower ordered the attack delayed by a single day to June 6th, 1944 in hopes to see if this might make a difference. Allied meteorologists gave him a somewhat optimistic report that a slackening of the storm might be coming. If accurate, the weather on June 6th would be decent, though not ideal, for the invasion to begin. Army planners and Ike knew the invasion had to happen no later than the 6th. The conditions for a seaborne landing would only be good until June 6th. The phase of the moon and ocean tides would be unfavorable after the 6th and favorable conditions would not come around again for another thirty days.

The delay of the invasion beyond June 6th would compel the thousands of ships to return to their harbors and disgorge their troops, costing millions of dollars, greatly affecting morale and possibly tipping off the Germans that the great invasion was coming.

As the day of the 5th progressed, the rain and wind did not slacken. Yet, the clock was ticking and Ike had to decide whether to give the order to "go" or "no-go" regarding June 6th. With great trepidation, he decided to trust the meteorologist's prediction. He gave the command; the invasion was on.

All these years later, we know the outcome of that invasion. Yet, there were so many variables that could have caused the invasion to be an utter failure. Ike knew that this was a very risky venture. And on the evening of June 5th, as Allied airborne divisions were already aloft and preparing to cross the Channel, as Allied ground troops were steaming nervously toward the coast of France in five thousand vessels, Ike sat in his quarters, chain smoking, drinking cup after cup of coffee, and watching the sheets of rain drench the windows of his office. Now he must await word on how the invasion was progressing. The invasion was now delegated to the men on the ground.

> *"When time comes to make a decision,…he must make it on his own responsibility and take full blame for anything that goes wrong."*
>
> General Eisenhower

An enlightened leader must be willing to take blame for things that go wrong. Even things that are out of his or her control, or things that have been delegated to others.

The chances of the invasion being a failure were just about equal to the chances of success. The outcome would be determined by factors Ike could no longer control. The tide of history was rolling and there was little or nothing Ike could do at this point but wait and worry.

Uncertain, he took a small piece of paper and wrote a very brief speech; a speech, thank the Lord, he never had to make. Yet one he was prepared to make. It said:

> *"Our landings in the Cherbourg-Havre area have failed to gain a satisfactory foothold and I*

have withdrawn the troops. My decision to attack at this time and place was based on the best information available. The troops, the air and the Navy did all that bravery and devotion to duty could do.

If any blame or fault attaches to the attempt, it is mine alone."

Ike was ready to take the fall for the failure of the invasion. He folded this small piece of paper and tucked it into his wallet. Some Eisenhower aides claim this unspoken speech stayed folded in his wallet, even into his presidency, as a reminder of what might have been.

How willing are you to take the blame for the failures of your subordinates? Many people, perhaps most people, would consider this a pointless folly and would be utterly unwilling to consider such an action. Yet enlightened leaders know the value of this.

Business leaders and supervisors often speak of "empowering' their employees". Yet employees are sometimes at best lukewarm to their leader's empowerment efforts. Through having been burned before, employees are often unwilling to accept the risks that come along with empowerment. Why? Because they don't trust their leaders. (It goes back to the issue of Integrity in Chapter 2)

Many companies encourage their employees to be "innovative" and "creative". Yet often, the reward for such innovation and creativity, when it goes wrong, is a verbal or written reprimand, or worse: termination. Such shortsighted actions by supervisors are guaranteed to ensure such mistakes will never happen again. Punishing those who fail while attempting to exercise "empowerment" or who try an innovative or creative solution succeeds only in stifling empowerment, innovation and creativity.

On the other hand, if the leader takes the blame for an employee's endeavor, that employee learns he or she is free to try new ideas. Businesses thrive on new ideas.

You want to free your employees to be innovative and empowered? Be loyal to them. Protect them. Cover their backs when they try something new.

And like I said earlier, if they do not succeed, is it failure? No, it is "feedback".

Decisiveness

The decision to attack on June 6th filled Eisenhower with anxiety. The conditions on June 5th were bad, with waves cresting to 16 feet. Carrying out an invasion under those conditions would have been disastrous. The meteorological reports of a slight lull in the storm on June 6th were professional guesses at best. But they were all Eisenhower had to go on. If the Allied invasion was delayed, the next favorable window with all the proper conditions of moon and tide would not come again until early July. Each day of waiting allowed General Rommel to further reinforce Fortress Europe, making the likelihood of a successful Allied invasion fade.

Ike had a difficult if not excruciating decision to make. Attack on June 6th and hope the weather reports are accurate. Or wait until early July and hope the enemy defenses would not become insurmountable.

Paralysis by Analysis

All leaders are, at some point, faced with nearly impossible choices. Sometimes the worst choice is inaction. None of us can see the future, but some of us believe that additional analysis of alternatives could give us a better understanding of the situation and potential consequences. Planning for alternatives is always helpful. But the trap of "paralysis by analysis" is something leaders or managers often get stuck in.

At "tipping point" moments, decisiveness is essential. There are times when a leader must decide. Sometimes, a bad decision is better than no decision at all. It at least gets the organization moving. And once it is moving, there is opportunity for adjustment.

Lack of decisions can bring an organization to a standstill. It can cause the decline of morale in an organization. And the more indecision, the more morale suffers.

When I was a young CPA with one of the national accounting firms, I ran into a situation where several of my supervisors were stuck in the paralysis by analysis syndrome. After our audit teams completed field work on certified audits, procedures and standards required a review of the field work by a "review manager" or a "review partner".

My department had a review manager and review partner that were infamous for indecision. Our audit teams worked hard on tight deadlines to complete client audits. We would bring the audits in on time and on budget only to see them sit in what we jokingly referred to as the "black hole". Being the early 1980s, there was a Paul Masson Wine commercial featuring Orson Welles. The closing line of that commercial in Orson Welles' famous baritone was "We will sell no wine before its time." Well that became our running joke. The audit teams quipped that our department would "release no audit before its time." Yet, it really was no joke.

The upside might have been that these very thorough reviews of the audits translated into a reduction in risk for the CPA firm. However the downside was that the timely work of the audit teams was neutralized by the long delays in review. This resulted in demoralization of our audit department.

While hasty decisions are a danger, indecision is also a significant danger. An effective leader must be one who reviews the data, considers the alternatives and potential outcomes and, putting fear aside, DECIDES. It is essential.

Chapter 8
An Enlightened Leader Encourages a Close, Family Relationship among Staff

As a football coach, Ike learned two key things about developing a successful and cohesive team:

1. Emphasize the team over a star, and
2. Coordination of effort rather than flashy individual performance. Doing so will usually lead to better results.

Eisenhower's staff clearly had some stars. Some demonstrated flashy performance as well. And while he encouraged independent action at the tactical level, he would never consider it at a strategic level.

Ike felt that for a team to truly function collectively, the leader must encourage a close family relationship among staff. At different times, Eisenhower shared his thoughts on these matters. His writings and quotes included ideas like:

- All departments must be a well coordinated team
- No successful staff can have any personal enmities existing
- A staff needs to be "one big crowd of friends"
- The Commander can have no personal enemies on the staff as it sabotages authority

Each of these sentiments indicates the closeness that Eisenhower thought was necessary for a team to function.

Ike also knew that the folks in the trenches feel a part of the team if they can see and talk with their leaders. Not just their direct supervisors, which should be a given, but with the folks higher up the chain of command.

Eisenhower said of commanders:

"...he must never lose touch with the ...troops. He can and should delegate tactical responsibility and avoid interference in the authority of his selected subordinates, <u>but he must maintain the closest kind of factual and spiritual contact with them or...he will fail.</u> This contact requires frequent visits to the troops themselves."

He also said,

"Nothing can take the place of direct contact between commanders and this is far more valuable when the senior does the traveling, instead of sitting in his headquarters waiting for subordinates to come to him."

In the following photos of Gen. Eisenhower, observe the Supreme Allied Commander's interaction with the troops. There was no grandstanding or military bluster in Ike. He just wanted to talk to the boys who were actually fighting and dying. He made an effort to visit every American and many Allied fighting units in the European Theatre of Operation. He didn't accomplish his goal, but he tried.

The photos all show a "good natured country boy" just talking to the troops. In most photos, there are smiles on the soldiers' faces as they speak to the top boss. In every photo, Ike is smiling. Ike felt renewed in meeting the troops. He learned much from them.

Today, we call what Eisenhower did "management by walking around" (MBWA). I don't believe there was a phrase for it in the 1940s. MBWA as a phrase was coined much later. That didn't stop Eisenhower. He understood the value of it intuitively.

Ike is always smiling!

Well, almost always smiling.

Meeting with one of HIS bosses, and close friend Prime Minister Winston Churchill, Ike's expression is...well, not quite a smile.

The Rest of the Story:
Ike Visiting the Troops in North Africa

Let me take you back to the opening story in this book. It is the story of Eisenhower going in an unguarded sedan to the front line troops in North Africa in late 1942 or early 1943. As Ike met the soldiers at the front, he became aware of a morale issue; a problem of which he had not been previously aware. As he dug further, he found that the morale problem was not one of defeats in the battlefield, or of malfunctioning equipment, or of lack of ammunition. The morale problem was caused by something much more fixable.

What Ike learned from the visit is the soldiers in the foxholes on the front lines could not get any cigarettes or chocolate. Now to you and me, that sounds like senseless griping about minor issues. Yet, when you are facing boredom and death, sitting unsheltered in the hot sun or pouring rain, small luxuries like a cigarette or a bar of chocolate take on mythic proportions.

After meeting with the soldiers, Ike promised to get to the bottom of the shortages.

Upon returning to Headquarters, Ike followed through on his promise. Ike could see from the men surrounding him at Headquarters and in Supply Services that there was no shortage of cigarettes and chocolate bars far back from the lines. He called the commander in charge of Supply Services to ask if there was a shortage of cigarettes or chocolate bars in North Africa. The officer assured Eisenhower there were warehouses full of them. When Ike asked why they were not being distributed to the troops in the field, the Supply Services commander reminded Ike that North Africa had only one meager two-lane paved road and one poorly maintained rail line crossing this vast land. He informed his commander that the single railroad and single paved road heading east to the front lines were already at or beyond shipping capacity with war essentials. He further explained that there was simply no room for non-essential items like cigarettes and chocolate.

Ike said, "That's fine, but I am writing a new order; until the soldiers at the front lines receive cigarettes or chocolate, no one in Supplies Services will be provided with cigarettes or chocolate."

Within weeks, cigarettes and chocolate were abundant at the front lines. Morale problem? Gone!

If Ike hadn't done his MBWA and personally met with the troops, at what point would the lack of cigarettes and chocolate and the resulting morale problem have been resolved? We can't know. But we can know that through MBWA, the Supreme Commander identified the problem and found a solution.

How often do you simply walk around to check in with your people? We're not talking about an inquisition or an investigation. We are not talking about overstepping the chain of command to fix problems under someone else's area of responsibility. We are talking about a sincere and friendly visit that allows a supervisor or leader an opportunity to take the pulse of the people who work for him or her.

Ike did his MBWA as frequently as possible. He was a man of duty first. Ike would work extraordinary hours to accomplish as much as possible during his work day. His staff was often worried about the level of stress he put his mind and body under in addition to the enormous stress his job naturally entailed. Ike did his duty to the fullest. But the work of the Supreme Commander is not the work that Ike loved. More than anything, he simply loved being with the soldiers in the camps, on the loading docks, on the airfields and at the front lines.

His salutation to the troops became his calling card: "Where are you from, Soldier?" This simple question often led to a heartfelt exchange with that soldier. The General was nourished by his contact with the men, but he learned a great deal from them as well.

On the afternoon of June 5th 1944, the day before the greatest amphibious invasion the world has ever seen, Ike wanted to visit as many of the soldiers taking part in the invasion as possible. He hurried his driver to the airfields where members of the 101st Airborne Division, the Screaming Eagles, were apprehensively waiting to load onto C-47 transport planes that would ferry them in the dark of night across the English Channel. These men would make up the advance waves of the Invasion of Normandy.

The airborne troops saw the staff cars arrive and wondered who was coming. To their surprise, out popped the Supreme Commander of the Allied Expeditionary Force, General Eisenhower. The men, fully loaded with equipment and many with faces already blackened with charcoal or shoe polish, gathered around the Supreme Commander.

Ike smiled at the waiting soldiers who were from the 502nd Parachute Infantry Regiment. The paratroopers quickly engulfed him. A tall, young lieutenant was standing directly in front of Ike. The famous photo of this encounter is found below.

Looking at this legendary photo, you may have formed an idea of what Ike is saying to the soldiers. With his fist raised and apparently pumping, it would appear he is saying "Go get 'em, boys!" or "Win one for the Gipper".

That's not at all what he was saying.

As this moment unfolded, Ike approached that tall, young lieutenant whose face was blackened like many of his comrades. Ike offered his hand in a handshake and asked his signature question, "Where are you from, Soldier?"

The young man shook the Supreme Commander's hand and said, "I'm from Michigan, Sir."

"Where about in Michigan?" asked Ike.

"Saginaw, Sir." The young man was Lt. Wally Strobel. I was told this story by his nephew, Mark Hoerauf, a member of the Board of Directors of a company our firm has assisted.

"I like Michigan," responded Ike. "I've been up there a couple of times to go fly fishing." Ike went on to try to describe the river he had been fishing on and the young lieutenant knew of it. Ike began to talk about fly fishing, one of his favorite hobbies. As Eisenhower talked to the men about the great fly fishing on that river, he became more animated. In this photo, his hand is raised, not pumping into the air, but holding an imaginary fly rod, casting on this distant river, in the land these men came from. The land these men loved.

Think of this: on the eve of the greatest amphibious invasion of all time, the Supreme Commander is among the first wave of troops who will jump behind enemy lines, and he is talking not about war or bravery or duty. He is talking about home! He is talking about the pastime of fishing that so many of these young men loved and would rather have been doing on this gloomy June day. Instead of adding pressure to these men who were already very keyed up, he is taking their minds off the stress and pressure of what they are heading into. He is not talking of the 80% casualty rate expected for these men, though he knew their odds. He was instead relaxing them so they would be ready. He was reminding them of their homes and the nation they were fighting for.

This is an enlightened leader!

Lieutenant Wally Strobel survived this jump and the war, he was one of the lucky ones. He died in 2003 having lived a full and productive life. But not many men of the 502nd survived Normandy as undamaged as Lt. Wally Strobel. Of the 792 men of the 502nd who jumped with Lt. Strobel that night, only 129 were able to walk out.

PRACTICAL APPLICATIONS ON DEVELOPING A CLOSE TEAM

How can a leader improve the closeness of a team? Often, simply knowing something about a colleague that you might not have known before can help you relate better to that colleague, identify experiences or interests you may have in common, or simply let you know that this person has a life outside of this office and had a life before they came to work here.

EXERCISE ONE
TELL US ABOUT YOU

With your management team gathered around, ask the team members to tell all of you some simple things about themselves, such as how many brothers and sisters they have, where they grew up, their favorite hobby, their first job, their worst job, where they studied, etc. Keep it easy and simple with this one, make sure it is nothing too personal, painful, or private to start. This is just a chance to practice this process.

As each person shares their story, fellow team members should be allowed to ask them questions or to share something similar. It is not the colleagues' time to tell their story yet. Allow each team member to have the floor.

Then move to the next team member and repeat the process.

The leader needs to facilitate this process and make sure that each person is protected and that their time is sovereign. If this discussion gets uncomfortable or too personal, decisively extinguish the discussion and move to the next team member. Remember, this is part of the "baby steps". Caution is a good idea.

EXERCISE TWO
TELL US SOMETHING WE DIDN'T KNOW ABOUT YOU

Again, with your management team gathered around, ask the team members to tell all of the team something they probably didn't know about them self.

This is a step beyond Exercise 1 and can go into more depth. But again, the leader needs to facilitate this process. If this discussion gets uncomfortable or too personal, decisively extinguish the discussion and move to the next team member.

EXERCISE THREE
HOW DO I SEE YOU

Now we are beginning to take risks. We are going to put each team member in the spotlight and ask each of the other team members to share something they respect or admire about the spotlighted team member. Don't pull this as a surprise. You will probably want to tell team members in advance to be prepared to share.

EXERCISE FOUR
TEAM PLAYER

The risk level has just gone up a notch. This is an exercise to do when the level of trust of the group is strong enough. Each team member is going to identify what they see as the one most important contribution that each team member makes to the team AND an area each of those team mates should work on to be a more effective team mate.

Once more, the team leader needs to monitor this and ensure it is a safe environment and that tact and diplomacy are demonstrated. Again, this shouldn't be a surprise.

Yet, while this may seem to be a chance to open up a can of worms, even teams that are not yet very effective can gain tremendously from this exercise. It requires compassion, respect and leaving your ego at the door.

Chapter 9
An Enlightened Leader
Remains Optimistic at All Times

Attitudes are contagious. This is an important psychological fact for all leaders to remember. The old expression "one bad apple can spoil the lot" talks about the effect that one pessimistic person or one person with a negative attitude can have on an entire team or organization.

Fortunately, the converse is true as well. One optimistic person or a person with a very positive, nothing-can-stop-me attitude can also affect an entire team or organization.

A pessimistic attitude is contagious, but so is an optimistic attitude. Further, both pessimism and optimism create self-fulfilling prophecies. You convince yourself that you can't do something and you are already condemned to failure. You convince yourself that you or your team CAN do something and you have just increased your chances of success exponentially. Optimism doesn't guarantee success, but it sure makes it more likely.

Sometimes in a business situation, we start a project with no assets other than pure optimism. This was one of the key attributes Gen. George Marshall saw in Dwight Eisenhower when he identified him as the future leader of the U.S. Army. He saw a man of endless optimism. This was truly essential at the start of the war as the U.S. had "nothing in excess but deficits."

In the early days of 1942, all Ike was armed with to take on the vaunted German war machine was optimism. Those who worked for Gen. Eisenhower began to realize that the attitude they exuded mattered. One said,

> *"Any expression of defeatism or any failure to push ahead in confidence was instant cause for relief from duty, and all officers knew it."*

Battle of the Bulge: Opportunity from Tragedy

Following the breakout of the beachhead at Normandy in August of 1944, Allied armies pushed rapidly across France and parts of Belgium. Vast portions of occupied Europe were liberated and the enemy was unable to slow the Allied advance.

As a result of much heavy fighting and remarkable supply systems, like the Red Ball Express that worked tirelessly to keep up with the rapidly expanding front, Allied forces, now nearing two million men strong, reached the German border. It was early September 1944.

The race across France and Belgium had been so easy and the collapse of the German army in France so complete that Allied soldiers at every level, from infantry in the fields to commanders in the headquarters, were confident that "We'll be celebrating Christmas in Berlin."

But as fall approached, German resistance stiffened. Allied forces suffered a humiliating defeat in the operation code name Market-Garden, Montgomery's poorly thought out and more poorly executed attempt to drive like an arrow through occupied Holland and over the Rhine into

Germany. Once German soldiers found themselves defending their homeland instead of occupied territory, the rapid advance of the Allied forces was slowed, then stopped.

Making the situation much easier for the German troops and much more difficult for the Allied troops was the established defensive works built at the German border in case of this eventuality. The Allies nicknamed this massive defensive frontier of Germany the Siegfried Line. This nearly impenetrable line of heavily fortified bunker systems with overlapping fields of fire and tank barriers slowed the mechanized forces and brought the Allied advance to a standstill.

By the end of September 1944, the race across France was halted. The war had come to a stalemate. Fighting didn't come to a standstill, not at all. Allied commanders tried again and again to breach the Siegfried Line. But enemy resistance was so great that the front lines hardly moved throughout the fall. Both Allied and enemy casualties mounted as the stalemate wore on.

Yet, the Allies were supremely confident that the enemy couldn't last much longer. Allied aircraft had control of the skies, German cities and industry were being bombed to rubble, and the enormous Soviet Red Army was threatening Germany from the east. All the Allies needed was one significant breakthrough and the war would soon be over.

This stalemate continued through October, November and into December, and enemy resistance held. As winter approached in northern Europe, conditions for an Allied advance into Germany began to deteriorate. But because of Allied air superiority and new Allied troops pouring onto the Continent, Allied commanders and men still waited for the big breakthrough.

Allied troops held a line that ran from Switzerland in the south, to Holland in the north. As winter neared, the number of Allied troops in northern Europe reached three million. Yet three million men over front stretching five hundred miles meant that the number of troops per mile was actually quite few. In order to dissuade the enemy from attempting a major counterattack, Eisenhower concentrated his troops in the lower, flatter areas where there were good road systems. This was based on playing the odds that the enemy would counter-attack in an area conducive to such an operation.

In the more rugged and under-populated areas of the line, Eisenhower's commanders placed few troops. In the Ardennes Forest of Belgium, which shared a border with Germany, the forest was thick, the roads were few and, as a result, fewer and greener troops were placed there. In some places, troops were in fox holes one hundred yards apart defending this quiet stretch of front line. The Allied Supreme Command saw very little danger of enemy activity in this unlikely frontier.

With air superiority, allied aircraft reconnoitering the area had not noticed any activity that would cause concern around the Ardennes Forest. Furthermore, Eisenhower and the Supreme Headquarters had concluded that the Germans didn't have anything left. They were stretched even more thinly than the Allies in manpower and equipment in the winter of 1944-45.

The Shock!

Then, in what was perhaps the greatest military intelligence failure of World War II, the German Army conducted a massive surprise attack. On December 16, 1944, 500,000 fresh German troops in brand new equipment, including hundreds of newly manufactured King Tiger tanks, attacked the lightly defended Allied front in the Ardennes Forest. These highly motivated enemy troops routed the green American soldiers who were totally unprepared for such an onslaught.

Soon, American troops, who had so confidently and effectively rolled up enemy opposition since Normandy, were running for their lives. Entire regiments were surrounded and captured in the first few days of the counter attack. Some American divisions, one of which was the newly organized 106th Division, were nearly destroyed.

Young soldiers, like private Dub Flowers of Georgia had never experienced battle and had certainly never endured 40 degree below zero weather. Dub was on the front line that morning of December 16th, when he saw the overwhelming German infantry and tanks rolling toward his foxhole. It became apparent in a matter of hours that defense was futile. With his officers and non-commissioned officers killed, captured or just lost in the forest, Dub found a group of soldiers and simply ran. Dub told me he ran for

Soldiers in heavy snow during the Battle of the Bulge

two weeks. The temperatures rarely rose above zero and never above freezing. His little group never knew where the Germans were, though he said they were everywhere, and never knew where the main body of the American Army was. When I met Dub, he was 86 years old. He limped over to me and said, "Did you see my limp, I am still on disability from the Battle of the Bulge. My feet were frostbitten so badly that I still can't walk right today."

Within days, the German army had punched a "bulge" 70 miles deep into Allied territory. Hitler's gamble in this winter offensive was that his army could push a wedge between British Field Marshall Montgomery's Army Group to the north and American Gen. Omar Bradley's Army Group to the south. Hitler felt that dividing the Allies might cause the Alliance to falter, providing his Government an opportunity to sue for a separate peace with the west rather than facing unconditional surrender.

Further, his Reich was nearly out of fuel. What little fuel was available was being shared by the defenders on both the eastern and western fronts. If the German army could reach the great Allied fuel depots located in Belgium, they could obtain the fuel needed to provide for continued resistance against the Allies.

For the first time since 1943, the Allies were on the retreat on a broad front. What appeared days earlier to be sure victory now saw Allied troops running for their lives from a reinvigorated enemy. Suddenly, the possibility of defeat at the hands of the Germans was looming.

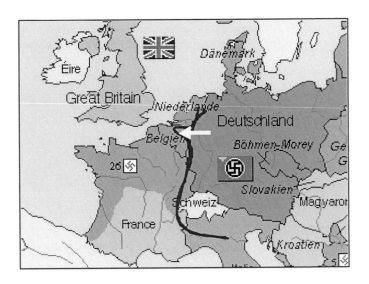

It took the Allied command several days to fully comprehend the enormity of the German counter attack. On December 18th, two days after the initial attack, Eisenhower convened a meeting of his commanders in Verdun, France, the scene of one of the bloodiest and longest battles of World War 1. All his senior commanders came. (except his top British subordinate, Field Marshall Montgomery, who would never condescend to coming to see Eisenhower, but who instead required Eisenhower to always come to him).

In this meeting, there was a profound feeling of pessimism. Allied commanders, who a few days earlier were expecting ultimate victory, were now seeing the very real possibility of defeat, or nearly as bad, a stalemate like World War 1.

As Eisenhower entered the room, he could see the glum faces. He could feel the palpable fear and concern. He could sense the cold atmosphere of defeat unlike anything his command had experienced before.

Then he looked at his subordinates and said sternly:

"The present situation is to be regarded as one of opportunity for us and not of disaster. There will only be cheerful faces at this conference table."

Gen. Eisenhower
Verdun, December 18, 1944

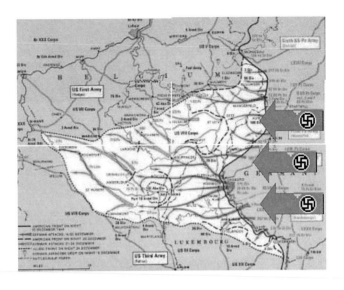

The Power of Optimism

Why would a commander treat his most senior subordinates in such a way? Why would he come into a room and tell them what expression would be allowed on each face? This behavior could certainly have been construed as condescending or micro-managing. It could also be construed as painting lipstick on a pig, namely, using window dressing to make a bad situation look less bad.

Neither of these were Eisenhower's intention. Ike was keenly aware of the power of *attitude*. He knew that by allowing a mood of pessimism to prevail, failure was nearly assured. He also knew that if he could provide a motivation to change the mood in the room to one of optimism, even a contrived optimism, good things may follow.

Both optimism and pessimism can become self-fulfilling prophecies. If Ike allowed his commanders to face this problem with a pessimistic attitude, the battle was already lost. A person's mind will act on the reality it is perceiving.

By conjuring an attitude of optimism, Eisenhower was able to elicit an entirely different set of possibilities. Optimism breeds creativity.

Optimism breeds creativity

If you believe you are already successful and have little doubt of it, your mind will find ways of creating the very success you believe in. We create much of what is around us. "You attract what you believe" is a phrase you may have heard. Of course, it is not quite as simple as that, but there is a great truth evidenced there. What you believe influences the reality you experience.

Changing the mood in that meeting room in Verdun was the result of Ike's force of will. He was saying to his commanders. This battle, the Battle of the Bulge, is already won. We just have to figure out how to do it.

Optimism breeds creativity. By facing a problem with optimism, you free your mind to search for creative responses to the problem. Through this flow of creativity, which is stifled by pessimism and negativity, solutions arise that might otherwise never be discovered. By saying "Woe is me, all is lost," you have sealed your fate. By saying, "I don't know what it is yet, but this cloud has a silver lining somewhere, and I am going to find it," you change the realm of possible.

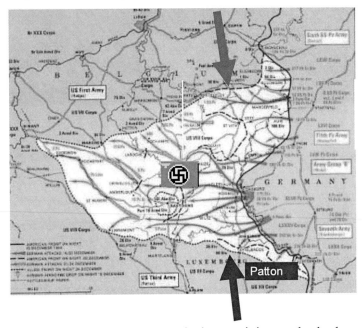

As the meeting progressed, the participants looked at a series of scenarios and solutions. All the commanders had been frustrated by their inability to break through the Siegfried Line over the last several months and the near World War I-level stalemate their troops were experiencing. Well, with this massive enemy attack, at least something had changed. The Allies were at least not stuck facing the Siegfried Line.

The Silver Lining in the Battle of the Bulge Cloud

It was at this point that Eisenhower's optimism paid off. Suddenly, Ike saw the silver lining in this massive enemy counter attack. He went to the map of the situation and began to share his idea. He showed the commanders the Siegfried Line, now far behind the enemy bulge, and shared his frustration that the Allied forces had been pounding their heads against this wall of steel and concrete for months with little to show for it. Ike acknowledged that Hitler's army had been well protected at the German border by this defensive bulwark.

Ike's pointer then traced a line around the bulge caused by the deep enemy advance. He explained that surprisingly, Hitler had exposed 500,000 men without a defensible perimeter. The answer was simple, it was right before them. All the Allies had to do was move part of Montgomery's Army Group southward and part of Bradley's Army Group northward and the Allies could cut off and defeat the 500,000 Wehrmacht troops.

With this, the attitude in the room shifted immediately. Gen. George Patton, one of Ike's closest friends, one of his most effective combat officers, and one of his most difficult subordinates, boasted "I can get my army moving northward in forty eight hours." Patton's Army was huge. But Patton said he could disengage six divisions, around 120,000 men and move them north. Moving an army of this enormous size would normally take much more than three days to organize. None of the officers around the table believed it at first, considering it just another example of Patton's bluster and grandstanding. But Patton defended his offer and said he could do it.

What only Patton knew was that he had previously ordered such a scenario plan developed in advance. As he left the room, he gave the order "Play Ball," which started the drive of six divisions northward even before he rejoined his command. It took a great deal more talking and a little more planning, though not much, and the two massive Armies began the process of changing direction and moving to cut off the massive German salient. Patton followed through on his claim and had his army moving through this frigid snow-covered, nearly roadless expanse of Belgian forest in two days. His troops reached the surrounded 101st Airborne Division on December 26th. This was a belated Christmas present for the 101st Airborne, which had been heroically defending the city of Bastogne. They thus delayed the German advance to the west.

The Battle of the Bulge waged on into the latter part of January. German casualties were enormous. Hitler's Wehrmacht lost 100,000 men in this last ditch effort to avoid "unconditional surrender". The German army defending its western border was crushed and Allied troops would shortly overrun Germany. The war would be over within a few months.

What to Do When Bad Things Happen

Very often in business bad things happen. Leaders have a choice of how to meet these disappointments. A person can complain and gripe and see all the bad in the situation. And this would probably not be inaccurate. There is often a great deal of bad in any difficult situation. And the bad is usually quite obvious. It is easy to focus on the bad.

Yet, it is an attitudinal choice that can often allow us to "snatch victory from the jaws of defeat". A leader can lead a group via a negative attitude to a slow, or sometimes rapid, demise. Or, by choosing an attitude of optimism, an enlightened leader can change the mindset of a team, helping the team focus on the possible.

Ike's method was to use an empowered staff as trusted colleagues in the planning process. By using the collective thinking of a bright and empowered staff, infused with enthusiasm, great results are often achieved.

> *"My method is to drag all disagreements into the open, discuss them frankly, and insist upon positive rather than negative action in furthering the purpose of Allied unity."*
> General Dwight D. Eisenhower

Each of us chooses our own attitude. Maybe you don't see it that way, but it is true. Your spouse may have angered you, a bad driver may have set you off, maybe you're ill or having financial problems. You may have strong reasons for behaving negatively or being pessimistic.

Yet the truth is, you decide how to react to any event. If you become angry because someone did something to you, you have handed control of your response to someone else; you have just lost your freedom. You have just become a puppet on a string for the person you allowed to anger you.

If you chose optimism and a positive, grateful attitude, you have retained control. You are in charge of how you will respond.

Optimism is a chosen attitude.

Optimism is a chosen attitude.

(No, that is not a typo. I have repeated it for emphasis. Are you getting the point?)

PRACTICAL IDEAS ON
REMAINING OPTIMISTIC AT ALL TIMES

As you arrive at work, stay in your car a moment.

1. Set yourself on a foundation of optimism, knowing that whatever comes your way, there is a positive solution. Say to yourself, "No matter what comes my way, I know we will find a solution." Close your eyes and repeat this at least ten times.

2. Remember, you as a leader are actually a servant. Say to yourself, "I am here to serve our customers (clients) and those who work for me. I am a servant leader." Again, close your eyes and say this at least ten times.

This focusing and reminder helps establish a solid foundation for how you start your day. It sets you up for positive, creative responses to all the coming day's events.

Gratitude Journal

Many people cannot see what there is to be optimistic about.

A very useful practice is to keep a Gratitude Journal.

Purchase a small notebook. Once each day, I suggest first thing in the morning or last thing in the evening, take time to write five things you are grateful for. Some days, it may be difficult or nearly impossible to identify things to be grateful for. That being the case, start with the basics: I am glad I had enough to eat today. I am glad it was sunny today. I am glad it was rainy today as the crops need the water.

This simple practice, done for one month, can do more to propel you to optimism and a good attitude than anything else.

Give it a try. You just might establish an attitude of gratitude and optimism.

Chapter 10
An Enlightened Leader
Deals Well with Difficult People

I'll bet none of the people you work with, work for, or who work for you is difficult. Yeah, right. Only in your dreams. By virtue of human nature and the laws of probability, we are guaranteed to run into someone, or several someones in our work that we find very difficult to deal with. An interesting addition to this is that often your most talented staff members can at the same time be some of your most difficult staff members. What do you do about that?

How you manage these relationships will often dictate your level of success as a leader. If you, as the leader, let a person get under your skin to such a degree that your response can easily be predicted (habitual response) or inevitably leads to anger (loss of control), you have handed your will to another person. This is a breakdown in leadership. By allowing this, you are letting the other person dictate your response.

An organization or group is better served by a leader with self control, one who responds from a grounded and creative space. Grounded in that he or she is not easily prodded into negative behavior by a difficult subordinate; creative in that his or her response is very appropriate and relevant to the situation. A creative and grounded response can often win over the most difficult person.

Eisenhower had no shortage of difficult subordinates. As a matter of fact, two of his most important generals, British Field Marshal Montgomery and 4 Star General George S. Patton, were among the oddest yet most effective subordinates Ike commanded.

Montgomery was beloved by the British population. In the early years of the war, when all of Europe had fallen to the Nazi war machine and England was being battered and fearing invasion, the British people were starved for a victory. Montgomery gave them that first victory.

After three years of war, in early 1942, German forces were on the verge of destroying all British resistance in North Africa and taking the British colony of Egypt. It was a relatively unknown British general, Montgomery, who led a decisive and well planned attack against the German Afrika Korps at El Alamein and drove them back to Tunisia. Thus Monty became a much loved and celebrated hero of the British people and that would not change during the war.

However, that love was not shared by everyone. His own Prime Minister, Winston Churchill, a man who desperately needed Montgomery, called Monty "A great man to serve under, a difficult man to serve with, and an impossible man to serve over." Another time, as noted earlier, Churchill described Monty as "The most irritating man in the Universe."

Why was Montgomery so difficult? Part of it was his confidence, which most interpreted as arrogance or cockiness. He was very self-focused.

Some years ago, I had the opportunity to meet an Englishman who had attended the Royal Military Academy Sandhurst in England in the 1960s. Sandhurst is the British equivalent of America's West Point. He told me a story that took place while he was there.

Retired Field Marshall Montgomery had come to Sandhurst to speak to the cadets. The cadets were well aware of Monty's propensity to focus on himself. So in advance of his speech, they created a pool betting on how many times Monty would use the pronoun 'I'. The former cadet I had the good fortune of meeting said he stopped counting after fifteen minutes as Montgomery had used "I" sixty five times surpassing all wagers. Montgomery's style of leadership was certainly different than Ike's.

You can imagine that a subordinate like this might have been difficult for Eisenhower to handle. Yet there is more. Montgomery refused to travel to Ike.

Whenever Ike ordered his commanders to come to him for a meeting, Monty would not come to Ike. He never directly refused an order, but instead would tell the Supreme Commander how buried he was in his work and how unfortunate it was that he would not be able to attend. In the spirit of Allied unity, which Ike saw as essential to the eventual victory over Nazism, Ike would always allow Montgomery this privilege. In order to maintain Allied unity, which was so key to the success of the war effort, Ike always traveled to Monty.

While Ike put up with this, it angered and frustrated him. Yet he never let that anger dictate the way he would lead, or even the way he would deal with this difficult employee. But it was a constant irritant for Eisenhower.

In one critical meeting between Eisenhower and Montgomery late in the war, Ike and his aide travelled to Monty for a "discussion". Monty met with the Supreme Commander in Ike's aircraft as Eisenhower had recently reinjured his damaged knee and was unable to walk. When Eisenhower's aide attempted to remain in the aircraft, Montgomery insisted he not be allowed to attend. Yet Montgomery's insisted his own aide be present. This nearly put Eisenhower through the roof but, again, in the spirit of Allied relations, Ike permitted this indignity.

In a recounting of this interaction, Montgomery and Eisenhower were seated directly facing each other. Because of the narrowness of the aircraft, the knees of the two men were nearly touching. In this confined space, the "most irritating man in the Universe" began to lecture and berate his commanding officer. Montgomery was very hot on some subject and clearly felt that Eisenhower, whom Monty had always seen as his inferior, was not up to the task. As he continued to lecture his commander in an extreme and demeaning way, Eisenhower's face turned several shades of red and the veins on his rather prominent forehead began to bulge.

Yet, rather than being goaded into losing his temper, which would have constituted a victory for Montgomery, Eisenhower composed himself and began to tap Montgomery's knee. Montgomery was unfazed by this attempted interruption for a bit, but eventually

Eisenhower's insistent tapping prompted Montgomery to stop and say in his high, nasal voice, "What is it?"

Ike, in a surprisingly calm but unambiguous voice, said,

> *Steady, Monty! You can't speak to me like that. I'm your boss."*

After that calm, measured, but clear reminder, Montgomery remained silent, sighed, and asked, "Yes, General, I apologize." In this single moment, Eisenhower had finally won Montgomery's respect as a leader. It had taken several years, but it finally happened. Their relationship would be different for the remaining months of the war.

Ike worked hard to be patient, yet decisive. He did his best to let others have their say. This was very helpful with all his subordinates, but it also did a great deal to win over his British subordinates. You may recall a quote from Chapter 1:

> *"It was inevitable Eisenhower would have his way. His real achievement was that he had won without alienating the British....He turned them down but only after giving them the opportunity to fully state their views, and he never let himself be provoked into losing his temper."*

Stephen E. Ambrose
"The Supreme Commander"

Decisive in Removing People Who Don't Work Out

Working with difficult people does not mean you must put up with difficult people, or people who are not working out. There may be times where putting up with difficult people is the right thing for the team and for the organization. On the other hand, difficult people can also destroy a team. A leader's discernment in these matters is critical.

If a leader allows a difficult person to damage the team or the organization, the leader is failing in his duty.

Holding staff accountable for both their results and their behavior is essential. When accountability declines in an organization, the sense of team deteriorates. If staff members do not live up to the stated standards of behavior or results, and yet are not held accountable, those who are producing or honoring high standards of behavior will become demoralized. When they become demoralized, they begin to lose confidence in their leader.

Eisenhower stated,

"The instant...commanders lose the confidence...of the majority of their principal subordinates, they must be relieved."

Repeatedly during the war, Eisenhower was faced with commanders losing the confidence of a majority of their subordinates. This often left him with difficult decisions as the American Army was very short of experienced officers. Each officer he lost was a real blow to his organization chart. Yet these decisions had to be made. Ike learned the hard way that they had to be made quickly too.

In chapter seven, I speak of Eisenhower's handling of Gen. Friedenhall in North Africa. This was early in Ike's command and he lacked confidence in himself and his judgment to be as decisive as required. This indecisiveness and reluctance to sack a commander who had clearly lost the confidence of his subordinates caused many British and American officers and soldiers to lose confidence in Ike's abilities as a commander.

An example of Ike's maturation as a commander occurred later in 1943. Gen. George Patton was one of the few American generals who was unafraid of being aggressive on the battlefield. Patton loved to attack and force his enemy to be on the defensive. Patton's theory was that, "The Germans can't shoot as well when they are on the run, so keep attacking." Eisenhower saw Patton as so important to the Allied strategy that he exclaimed, "I cannot win this war without Patton leading one of my Armies."

To complicate the issue with Patton, Patton had been one of Ike's early mentors and senior officer in the pre-war Army. Patton taught Ike everything Ike knew about tank warfare when he was under Patton's command at the tank school in Gettysburg, Pennsylvania years before.

Ike and George were very close personal friends who had spent a great deal of personal time together before and occasionally during the war. The very modest and understated Eisenhower and the very flashy, self-aggrandizing, foul mouthed Patton were seen as an odd couple, but close they were.

During Patton's rapid advance through Sicily during Operation Husky in 1943, an incident occurred that forced Eisenhower to take an action that he absolutely hated to take.

In a visit to a hospital to award Purple Hearts to wounded soldiers, Patton came upon a soldier with no apparent wounds. Today, the soldier would be diagnosed with severe Post Traumatic Stress Syndrome. The period diagnosis was Battle Fatigue. Patton would have none of this psychoanalytical babble and called the soldier a coward and slapped the dumbfounded man.

This incident was witnessed by the medical staff and war correspondents who were appalled by the treatment. Word got out to Patton's division, causing widespread dissent among his soldiers. Eventually word of this got back to the Supreme Commander who had to act. In a telephone call to his subordinate, Ike told Patton how severely disappointed he was in this behavior. He ordered Patton to assemble his soldiers and apologize to them, which Patton grudgingly did. Yet this was still not enough. Eisenhower realized that the discontent among the officer corps and enlisted men, not to mention the growing uproar in the States, was growing out of control. Reluctantly, yet decisively, Ike fired Patton.

The firing of Patton and losing arguably the Army's most effective general put the troops at a certain disadvantage. But failure to do so would have been dereliction of duty by the Supreme Commander.

Patton's war was not over, not by a long shot. Ike would shelter him and hide him, using him as a decoy in Great Britain to keep the German's occupied wondering where Patton was and where Eisenhower was going to use him next. And in June of 1944, shortly after D Day, Patton would take his vaunted 3rd Army across the English Channel to Normandy and drive aggressively into the heart of the enemy, proving once again to be one of America's most formidable combat leaders.

Leadership and Radical Trust

One of Eisenhower's great attributes was his sincere enjoyment of people. This simple country boy truly trusted people. Many people have the belief that it is best to distrust people until they prove themselves trustworthy. For a leader, the potential disadvantage in this attitude is the leader is always watching people for evidence to either prove their bias or to prove that this time their bias might be wrong. Since the leader doesn't trust his subordinates, delegating to them can be difficult. Furthermore, each failure by a subordinate becomes evidence of the leader's bias and each success may be passed off as luck or an exception.

On the other hand, Eisenhower believed all people to be honest and trustworthy unless convinced otherwise by experience. This allowed for an open and trusting relationship from the very beginning.

Eisenhower believed all people to be honest and trustworthy unless convinced otherwise by experience

People often live up to other's expectations of them. By Eisenhower treating people as honest and trustworthy, they, perhaps, were reluctant to let him down. Eisenhower may simply have treated others as he saw himself, honest and trustworthy. Regardless of the reason, this approach can be very helpful.

When I was 16 years old, I suffered from lack of confidence and belief in myself. I suppose this is a common affliction of adolescence. My older brother Chuck was engaged to a lovely college classmate of his, Marci (still happily married nearly forty years later). Marci was from northern Mexico and had studied at Gonzaga University in Spokane, Washington where she and Chuck were classmates.

Just prior to their wedding which took place in Cananea, Sonora, Mexico, I was helping Marci's father, Hector Felix. He was a successful small businessman and I had a deep respect and admiration for him. I assisted Hector in several chores in preparation for the wedding and reception. On the afternoon before the wedding, as I was loading cases of soda into his pickup truck, a friend of Hectors saw us by the truck in the driveway and stopped to visit. Hector introduced me to the visitor then said to him, "I have learned that if you need to get something done, this young man Tim is the person to give it to."

I was flattered and surprised by this compliment. I had never thought of myself as an especially effective worker, at least not until that moment. With those few words from someone I admired and respected, my view of who I was and what I offered others changed. I was no longer "Tim, the lazy sixteen year old"; I was now "Tim, the person who you can trust to get things done." My self-view had changed forever. All these years later I can still remember that moment, that sunny afternoon in Hector's driveway in a little town in Mexico, and how significantly it impacted me.

I'm still not sure Hector's comment was true or accurate, because frankly, I don't think I had been all that helpful or responsible around Hector. But Hector's unequivocal expression of confidence and trust in me changed my reality. I thought of myself differently and I wanted to live up to what Hector saw in me.

On the other hand if Hector had said, "Well, don't expect Tim to help you. He's worthless. We're getting this done in spite of Tim," I likely would have lived up to that expectation instead. That would have become my reality. Employees, co-workers, even children regularly live up to expectations of them…or down to them.

You might say Ike's approach of radical trust is naïve. It is true, not all people are honest and trustworthy. By starting with this assumption, a leader is leaving himself open to being taken advantage of. Of course you can be taken advantage of by leading with this assumption. Eisenhower simply saw that the law of averages were in his favor. He believed that most people are, in fact, honest and trustworthy, and by starting with this assumption, he was able to expand his pool of reliable subordinates rapidly. If a subordinate did not prove to be trustworthy or reliable, he would respond appropriately.

One incident was not usually adequate for Eisenhower to change his mind about a person's honesty and trustworthiness. Ike had to be convinced. Therefore, it might take several failures of honesty and trustworthiness for Ike to be convinced. Once he become convinced, he was decisive in removing that subordinate.

There was one area, though, where Eisenhower's tolerance was not to be tested. It was in the area of relations with the British or other Allied personnel. If an American officer was found to be insulting or badmouthing his Allied counterparts, his time in the European Theatre of Operations would be short. Eisenhower summarily sent several American officers back to the States due to a single incident of offending Allied personnel. Allied unity was an area of such importance in Ike's eyes that he had a zero tolerance policy.

Relationships as Intensely Interesting

One of Ike's personality traits that helped him stay very centered and grounded during his time as Supreme Allied Commander was that he looked upon relationships as challenges and found them intensely interesting. Therefore, what some would see as personality struggles with others, Eisenhower found to be fascinating challenges.

No matter how bitter a struggle over an issue became, Ike was able to maintain good personal relationships. He had the ability to depersonalize an issue and see it as an object separate from the person. This ability often allowed him to look at an issue dispassionately rather than become entangled with the personality.

Leaders Don't Need to Treat All Subordinates Alike

Another key in understanding Eisenhower's success as a leader was that he DID NOT treat all people alike. Fair leadership does not mean standardized treatment of subordinates. As a matter of fact, an effective leader can sometimes be a bit of a chameleon when it comes to treatment.

Ike, Monty and other Allied Officers

In order to get the most out of people, a leader might identify what motivates individuals. Different things motivate different people. Treating everyone the same can diminish a leader's effectiveness.

On the other hand, a leader cannot be perceived as inconsistent or playing favorites either. These too can lead to a collapse of morale and trust. Therefore, discernment by a leader is crucial.

Eisenhower understood that certain people required special handling. Not based on favoritism. Rather, it was focused on achieving the VISION. Some of his most difficult subordinates were highly talented people who required special handling: Patton and Montgomery for instance. Eisenhower treated them differently, because they were especially talented. What they brought to the team was something that was difficult to duplicate; and their effectiveness or usefulness to the end result exceeded their liabilities to the organization.

Yet, I believe it is true, sometimes highly talented people require special handling. Great genius or talent often brings with it special personality quirks.

Providing special treatment, of course, can be very tricky and even dangerous to the organization. Every leader has to weigh benefits against liabilities and ask him or herself, "On balance, is this talented person with the odd behaviors a net asset or liability to this organization?"

Furthermore, it needs to be clear to the members of the organization that this is not "favoritism". It is simply exploiting the talents of some for the benefit of the organization.

PRACTICAL IDEAS ON
DEALING WITH DIFFICULT PEOPLE

Accountability is essential. An enlightened leader must hold employees responsible for their behaviors. Nothing hurts organization morale more than tolerating employees who do not deliver results or who undermine the organization's culture or values, yet are allowed to remain.

Be clear and consistent in rewarding employees for acceptable behavior and publicly discourage behaviors that undermine the culture or values.

Be cautious in making exceptions, as exceptions may be viewed as the leader's indifference to living by the culture or values.

CORPORATE CULTURE GRID

Cultural 'Competence' and Fit

	HIGH	LOW
HIGH	High – High **1**	Low – High **2**
LOW	High – Low **3**	Low – Low **4**

Technical Competence

However, too many organizations are willing to put up with a poor cultural fit because they desire to have people with adequate technical ability.

But leader after leader, when looking back on their career will tell you, "the biggest mistake I made in business was keeping people who were technically competent, but unable to fit into our culture" (or who couldn't get along with co-workers, or who were abrasive, or who lacked diplomatic skills, etc.). They will often focus on the human relations and corporate cultural skills.

Using the Corporate Culture Grid

Box 1: High –High:
High in the Culture and Values and High Technically. Promote them and empower them as much as you can. This is a competent team player. You can build a very successful business around this type of person

Box 2: Low-High:
Low in the Cultural Competency but High in the Technical skills. This is the kind of person who can quickly sap the lifeblood of an organization. Remove them as quickly as possible and fully explain to the staff why they were removed. This helps emphasize that weak Corporate or Cultural values will not be tolerated.

Box 3: High-Low:
High on the Cultural Competency but Low on the Technical skills and abilities. Educate them, give them a

second and maybe a third chance to succeed. Consider finding a new position in the organization for them where they might fit better. If all that fails, remove them.

Box 4: Low-Low:

Low on the Cultural Competency and Fit AND low on Technical Competency. Remove them as quickly as possible. No use harboring them for any reason.

There are at least three reasons why you would need to let an employee go. Remember that clarity, fairness and decisiveness are important to retain the trust and confidence of your staff.

1. For violations of integrity: Do it quickly and let people know why they were removed.
2. Due to poor financial performance of the company or economic conditions: Be sure your staff knows how the company is doing. Share financial data. Employees have a better chance of understanding if they have been informed along the way.
3. For lack of performance or poor cultural fit:
   Make sure employee has been informed along the way of his or her performance (no surprises)
   a. Standards should be clear and understandable
   b. Performance failure should be documented and the employee should acknowledge the documentation in writing
   c. Face-to-face performance evaluations and discussions are critical

When you have to let people go, don't avoid it. Letting an employee go is never easy, but it comes with the job. Delaying the inevitable can lead to a breakdown in morale as other employees wonder why "that person" can get away with not performing or meeting standards.

Chapter 11
An Enlightened Leader is Humble: Deflects Praise to Others

Humility is often misunderstood. Many people think of "humiliation" when they hear the word "humility." Humility, or humbleness is a virtue; a strength.

Humility is not thinking less of your self.
Humility is thinking of your self less.

In Chapter Three; I shared some of Ike's ideas on which officers would not be eligible for promotion. Note that three of them, the three listed below, have to do with ego-centered leaders:

• Self-seeking
• Great love of the limelight
• Treats subordinates as lesser

Ike had confidence. Ike had a presence. Ike liked people and in return, people liked Ike. People noticed Ike. As the war wore on and Allied forces achieved slow but steady success in Europe, Ike attained star status. Maybe we should call it "superstar" status.

Many American generals loved the status that came with their gold stars. Some, like Patton, lived for the limelight. Some, like General Mark Clark, mockingly nicknamed Marcus Aurelius Clarkus, were practically brought down by their desire for attention and fame.

But not Ike. He neither avoided nor sought attention. He simply faced his commanders, his subordinates, his soldiers in the field, the media and the general public as the kid from Kansas. He never thought of himself as something special. Yet, neither did he see himself as undeserving.

As a matter of fact, aside from helping in the design of a rather physique-enhancing officer's jacket, known as the Eisenhower Jacket, Ike had little ego invested in what he did. He simply served his nation as well as he knew how. To Eisenhower, service was everything.

Ike worked very hard. Ike missed many hours of sleep. He spent years away from his wife and son. All this to serve his nation.

After the war, Ike became the President of Columbia University, the Supreme Commander of NATO, and, well, the President of the United States. Ike didn't really seek any of these posts. What he really wanted was to return to his little farmhouse in Gettysburg, Pennsylvania and fish.

One of his key assets was a barely evident ego. He didn't envy the success of his classmates when they were sent to fight in the First World War while he stayed home. He was disappointed with his lack of field command, but not envious. He didn't envy the more rapid promotions of his fellow officers and their important roles as commanders of troops while he coached football teams and went to war planning schools. He again was disappointed at what he was not able to experience, but he wasn't envious.

He was never too important to learn from others like General Douglas MacArthur, from whom he learned how NOT to do things, and from General Fox Connors, who Ike idolized and from whom he soaked up wisdom like a sponge. Because he was not too proud to learn, he learned a great deal.

His humility allowed him to meet presidents and sailors, prime ministers and airmen, kings and soldiers: and treat them all as equals. He did not bow to the mighty, nor tower above the modest. At all times, he was just the hayseed from Kansas.

His humility was perhaps most evident in what Ike says here:

> A leader must *"be self-effacing, quick to give credit to others, ready to seek and take advice, and willing to decentralize....When time comes to make a decision,...he must make it on his own responsibility and take full blame for anything that goes wrong."*

As we said earlier, Eisenhower sought the counsel of large groups of subordinates before making a decision. He asked for opinions and considered dissent. While he canvassed and sought input, he was still decisive. While the process of preparing for a decision was quite democratic, decisions themselves were not a democratic process. He accepted the responsibility of making difficult decisions. But he rarely made them without talking to and listening to many subordinates.

While he made decisions himself, he did not draw the limelight to himself when those decisions were successful. And when he delegated decision-making to subordinates, and those decisions resulted in failure, he did not attempt to cast blame upon those who made the decision.

Regarding this matter Ike said:

> *"It's amazing what you can accomplish if you give others credit for it."*
>
> Eisenhower

Many bosses are too unaware or too self-centered or too insecure to give others credit for their successful ideas. In order to impress superiors, many a supervisor has intentionally or inadvertently taken credit for the work of his staff.

I've been present at meetings where a CEO has taken credit in front of his or her Board for a successful idea that came from one of the Vice-Presidents sitting in the Board room. Each time, the Vice-President visibly deflated and the other VPs cast sympathetic glances at the Vice-President. In each of those moments, the CEO shrank in stature in the eyes of the staff. The CEO's personal capital was severely depleted and his or her ability to lead by inspiring others to want to follow declined dramatically. You can bet his or her management team never fully trusted their CEO again.

Personal capital, like business capital, takes a long time to build and, unfortunately, very little time to deplete. A single lapse in integrity can destroy years of hard work.

Trust is slowly earned but is quickly lost if someone exhibits untrustworthiness.

Now, on the other hand, think about a true leader and how they deflect praise. Over the decade from 2000 to 2010, two professional quarterbacks have stood out as superb leaders of successful teams: Tom Brady of the New England Patriots and Payton Manning of the Indianapolis Colts had astounding success on the field. Both were prolific passers, sometimes astounding the fans with their magnificent skills. Both encountered what appeared to be insurmountable odds and led their team to victory. Yet in interviews, when reporters asked about some incredible passing statistic or a play that seemed to defy the laws of physics, both Brady and Manning quickly deferred the praise to their linemen who kept the defenders at bay and to their receivers who somehow got open or made a ballet like catch, or to the defense that stopped the opposing team to secure the victory. No matter how hard the reporters tried to get Manning or Brady to take credit, both men worked just as hard to deflect the praise to their co-workers.

In doing so, both men are 1) sharing a reality that no one succeeds alone, and 2) ensuring future success because they once again endeared themselves in the hearts of their co-workers by remembering them and their efforts.

No person is a success by him or herself. Every "self-made" success has relied on workers who did the labor, bankers who financed the business, police who kept the peace, schools that educated the employees, truckers who shipped goods, crews that built the roads and the list can go on and on. The person who forgets the contributions of others may be a boss, but will never be a leader.

As noted in Chapter 10, British Field Marshall Bernard Law Montgomery tested Eisenhower's leadership skills and patience like no other. Ike never let his behavior be controlled by Monty's insubordination or haughtiness. Ike always controlled his responses and remained in control of the situation. It took Eisenhower years, but he eventually earned the respect even of the irritating Field Marshall.

Shortly after the war, Montgomery wrote:

"Dear Ike:

...I would like to say what a privilege and an honor it has been to serve under you. I owe much to your wise guidance and kindly forbearance. I know my own faults very well and I do not suppose I am an easy subordinate; I like to go my own way. But you have kept me on the rails in difficult and stormy times, and have taught me much. For all this I am very grateful."

Monty

No Monty, you were not an easy subordinate. But even Monty's challenge to Ike was not enough to cause Ike to stray from his core values.

Enlightened leadership wins every time.
Let's look once again at the Traits of an Enlightened Leader.

An Enlightened Leader

- Exhibits personal integrity
- Plans thoroughly and communicates the vision clearly
- Selects staff well and backs them completely
- Encourages a close, family relationship among staff
- Remains optimistic at all times
- Deals well with difficult people
- Is humble and deflects praise to others

So I ask you,
who would you rather follow into the fray?

**Field Marshall Von Rundstedt of
the German Army Group West?**

Or
This guy who looks a little bit like Mickey Mouse?

And where does Enlightened Leadership Lead?

German General Jodl arriving to sign the Unconditional Surrender and the Third Reich resulting in the end of Hitler's Nazism. Gen. Jodl was found guilty of Crimes Against Humanity and executed.

And Ike?

Well, he became 34th President of the United States

In March of 1969, after a life of humility, service and unbounded success, Ike's big heart finally stopped beating. At the age of 79, one of America's Enlightened Leaders passed on to his eternal reward.

[1] An embellished account of an incident recounted by Eisenhower in his book *Crusade in Europe*, page 315

[2] *Eisenhower, Soldier and President*, Stephen E. Ambrose, p. 26`